Delhi
Agra Jaipur

Third Edition 2005
Prakash Books India (P) Ltd.
1, Ansari Road, Daryaganj, New Delhi-110 002
Ph: (011) 2324 7062-65. Fax: (011) 23246975
E-mail: sales@prakashbooks.com
Website: www.prakashbooks.com

Delhi Agra Jaipur

Surendra Sahai

PRAKASH BOOKS

CONTENTS

INTRODUCTION

There is a great need for a book which deals with the monuments of the cities of Delhi, Agra and Jaipur in detail. Visitors who are short of time and yet wish to know something about the legendary architectural wealth of the region may find this book useful.

After 1193, when the Rajput forces led by Prithvi Raj Chauhan III, the last Hindu ruler of Delhi, lost to the Turkish soldiers of Mohammad Ghori, a change took place in the architectural styles of the capital. The Hindu era ended with the ascendance of the Delhi Sultanate, followed by a violent clash of ideals and convictions. This culminated in the grand synthesis of a new composite style of Indo-Islamic architecture, which shows itself at its best in the monuments of Delhi and Agra.

The native artisan acquitted himself admirably well. The hands which had worked wonders on the stone surfaces of temples took little time to perfect the art of ornamenting with arabesque and calligraphic designs of the monuments built by the Delhi Sultans.

Delhi contains some excellent specimens of Indo-Islamic architecture: the Qutb Minar – an admirably sculptured gateway; the Tughlaqabad fort – a magnificent citadel built in rugged surroundings; the Red Fort – an example of grand palace architecture; the Jama Masjid – a simple but majestic royal mosque, Delhi has been the coveted capital of many empires. Battles over possession of the city have left it a mere skeleton of its former splendour but enough remains to bear testimony to its rich and glorious past. If there is any place in India which presents a panorama of 3000 years of continuous habitation and centuries of architectural activity, it is Delhi.

Agra contains almost as many splendid monuments as Delhi. It was the capital of the Lodis and the early Mughal emperors. During Akbar's rule, Agra prospered. The buildings at Agra and Sikri were among the greatest achievements of Mughal architecture. The transition from red sandstone to white marble coincided with the passing of power from Akbar to Jehangir and Shahjahan. The massive bastions and grand masculinity of the Agra Fort palaces, the visionary idealism behind the Sikri structures, the combination of red sandstone and white marble at Sikandara, the grandeur of *pietra dura* at Itmad-ud-daula and the Taj Mahal – the world's most famous garden tomb make Agra extraordinarily rich in architectural wealth.

Jaipur comes across as different and alluring. The capital of Rajasthan contains splendid examples of forts and palaces such as the Jaigarh fort, mysterious with massive walls and boasting of Jaivan, the world's largest cannon. There is Amber, a romantic palace with enchanting glass mosaics and spectacular *jali* screens. The City Palace where medieval elegance mingles with modern sophistication; and the Jantar Mantar – with primitive yet fascinating instruments for tracking heavenly bodies.

These monuments at Delhi, Agra and Jaipur are best appreciated when a visitor understands their history and significance. This book attempts to do that, both for the visitor in a hurry and for those with leisure. It tells you in adequate detail about the monuments and relates them to their place in the great architectural traditions of India.

Opposite page: Peacock doorway, Pritam Chowk, City Palace, Jaipur.

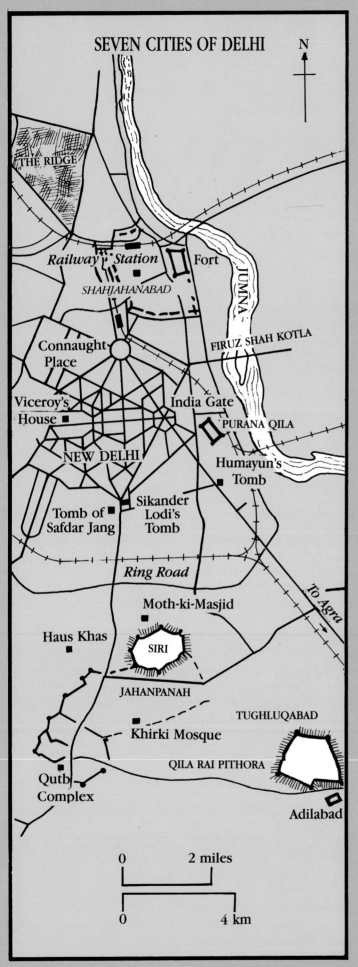

SEVEN CITIES OF DELHI

N

THE RIDGE

Railway Station   Fort

SHAHJAHANABAD

JUMNA

Connaught
Place

FIRUZ SHAH KOTLA

Viceroy's
House

India Gate

PURANA QILA

NEW DELHI

Humayun's
Tomb

Tomb of
Safdar Jang

Sikander
Lodi's
Tomb

Ring Road

To Agra

Moth-ki-Masjid

Haus Khas

SIRI

JAHANPANAH

TUGHLUQABAD

Khirki Mosque

QILA RAI PITHORA

Qutb
Complex

Adilabad

```
0           2 miles
|_____|

0           4 km
```

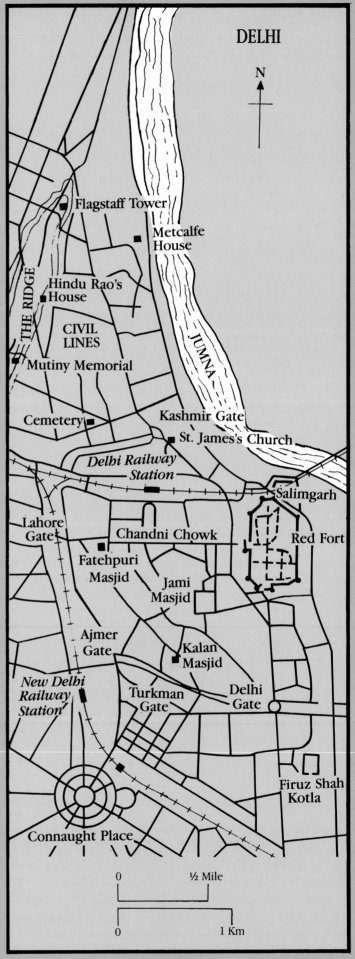

DELHI

N

Flagstaff Tower

Metcalfe
House

THE RIDGE

Hindu Rao's
House

CIVIL
LINES

JUMNA

Mutiny Memorial

Cemetery

Kashmir Gate

St. James's Church

*Delhi Railway
Station*

Salimgarh

Lahore
Gate

Chandni Chowk

Red Fort

Fatehpuri
Masjid

Jami
Masjid

Ajmer
Gate

Kalan
Masjid

*New Delhi
Railway
Station*

Turkman
Gate

Delhi
Gate

Firuz Shah
Kotla

Connaught Place

```
0           ½ Mile
|_____|

0           1 Km
```

8

Delhi
The City of Cities

Delhi is one of the most ancient cities of the world. Empires were built on it and destroyed, and then rebuilt by others. All these dramatic events have left their mark on the fabric of the city. The Rajputs, Turks, Afghans, Mughals and the British all fought for the possession of Delhi. They built their forts and palaces and often settled down permanently. Before long, however, they were replaced by others. Delhi assimilated them all and remained impassive to the vicissitudes of fortune, survived invasions, plunder and massacres and yet, like the phoenix, rose again in new splendour. "Its history is no less the story of India's than it is the history of the whole of Asia.... for centuries its splendour turned the heads of the Western world. If Rome was the centre of ancient Europe, Delhi was the metropolis of Asia," says Count Hans Von Koenigsmarck.

We know for certain that apart from the legendary city of Indraprastha, at least seven other prominent cities have stood at different times on the soil of Delhi. Ruins of these seven cities–Mehrauli, Siri, Tughlaqabad, Jahanpanah, Firozabad, Dinpanah or Shergarh and Shahjahanabad – built by the Turks, Khiljis, Tughlaqs, Afghans and Mughals can still be clearly identified.

Indraprastha The oldest of them is believed to be Indraprastha, the capital of the Pandavas in the great Hindu epic, the *Mahabharata*. The site of the Purana Qila is where that ancient capital is said to have risen to great fame and prosperity. A village of that name existed when the forces of Muhammad Ghori conquered Delhi in 1192. So far no archaeological evidence has been uncovered in support of the claims regarding the existence of Indraprastha, but as the historian, K. A. Narain observes: "Just as in the West the imagination of Homer became concretized through archaeological findings, it is now hoped that archaeological evidence will confirm literary evidence about Delhi. In fact, a beginning has now been made." With each new relic unearthed at the excavations on the site at Purana Qila, we move nearer to some solid incontrovertible evidence. After the glorious days of the Mahabharata era, Delhi fell into oblivion and survived as a mere insignificant adjunct of powerful cities like Mathura, Kannauj, and Pataliputra. Yet for centuries it withstood the ravages of time with fortitude.

Figurine and Coin from Purana Qila Excavation.

When the Tomars held Delhi in the tenth and eleventh centuries, they first stayed near Indraprastha and then settled at Anangpur near Tughlaqabad. There they built Suraj Kund, Delhi's earliest surviving structural monument. When they moved to the Mehrauli area, they built Lalkot, Delhi's first fortress. Hereafter, in terms of history and dates we are on surer ground. The Chauhans defeated the Tomars around 1056 and extended the walls of the city with fortifications including Lalkot within its northern limits. This was Qila Rai Pithora, named after the illustrious king Prithvi Raj Chauhan III. Ruined portions of the fort walls, bastions and ramparts, tanks and towers still survive amidst a wilderness of stones around the Qutb Minar.

Mehrauli In 1192 Muhammad Ghori's Turkish soldiers defeated Prithvi Raj Chauhan III. Ghori departed, but left behind his slave general Qutbuddin Aibak, stationed at Inderpat, or Indraprastha. The Mehrauli area was known as Yoginipura when Aibak entered Lalkot the following year. A temple dedicated to Yogmaya still stands near the Qutb. The early Sultans of Delhi built a few grand palaces south of the Qutb, but used the Qila Rai Pithora with its reinforced bastions and gates as their defence fort. The city of the Tomars and Chauhan Rajputs survived, though in a new form as the seat of the Delhi Sultanate.

For nearly a hundred years Mehrauli enjoyed royal favours, but then, following the consolidation of the empire and accumulation of treasures, plans were made to build a new township. Balban's grandson, Kaikubad, built a new city Kilokhiri, in 1287, on the banks of the Yamuna near Inderpat village. But it was used mainly as a pleasure haunt. Mehrauli still retained its status as capital of the Sultanate.

Siri Then came Ala-ud-din Khilji, who in 1303 built Siri between Kilokhiri and Mehrauli. This fort and its palaces have all been destroyed by his successors. Only some portions of its great walls have survived and can be seen near Siri Fort Auditorium and Shahpur Jat village.

Tughlaqabad Among the Tughlaqs, who were fierce and powerful Sultans, Ghiyasuddin, during the four years of his rule between 1320-24, built Delhi's most spectacular fort and a city named after the dynasty – Tughlaqabad. Muhammad Tughlaq abandoned Tughlaqabad, which was not yet fully completed, to found his own fort, Adilabad, on an adjacent hillock.

Jahanpanah Muhammad Tughlaq also started work on a city, Jahanpanah, surrounded by the walls of the cities of Mehrauli, Siri and Tughlaqabad, but it was never fully completed.

Firozabad The third Tughlaq, Sultan Firoz Shah, chose for his city a spot north of the existing settlements. This is called Kotla and stands on the banks of the river Yamuna. The perennial problem of water shortage in the cities of his predecessors was solved instantly. Firozabad prospered till Timur descended on the city in 1398, plundering and destroying Delhi at will. The city was reduced to ruins.

The Sayyads and the Lodis succeeded the Tughlaqs. They built no new forts. The Sayyads built Mubarakabad near Okhla, but not the faintest trace can be found of that structure today. The Lodis preferred to stay at Agra and when Babur defeated Ibrahim Lodi in 1526 near Panipat, he merely came and saw the monuments of Delhi before going to Agra.

Dinpanah and Shergarh Humayun decided to build Dinpanah, a new city on the site of Indraprastha. He hardly had time to raise the great walls when he was overthrown by the Afghan, Sher Shah, who quickly demolished Humayun's buildings and built Shergarh (1545-50), on the site of Humayun's city. Humayun returned to power, destroyed much of his adversary's work in turn and resumed his plans for Dinpanah, but died in 1556 within six months of his return to power.

Shahjahanabad Akbar, Jehangir and Shahjahan stayed at Agra. Then, in 1639, Shahjahan laid the foundations of a great new city on the bank of the Yamuna in Delhi, Shahjahanabad – the massive fort and the walled city was completed in 1648 and Delhi became the capital in an era of magnificence.

New Delhi Between 1857 and 1911, the British functioned from Calcutta as their capital. In 1911, for cultural and political reasons, Delhi regained its status as capital of British India. A new city was built outside the walled city of the Mughals.

Thus kingdoms rose and fell on the plains of Delhi and the fortunes of the city rose and fell with its rulers. The lure of Delhi remained irresistible, for it was realized long ago that Delhi held the key to India. He who held Delhi, it was believed, ruled India. Its strategic position made it the most logical choice as the country's capital and the river Yamuna on one side and the escarpment of the Aravalli Ridge on the other provided it with an efficient natural defence.

The Qutb Minar and Delhi Sultanate Architecture 1192, the year of the Turkish conquest of Delhi, was of immense significance not only in the architectural development but also in the cultural history of north India. "Seldom in the history of mankind," Sir Wolseley Haig observes, "has the spectacle been witnessed of two civilisations so vast and so strongly developed yet so radically dissimilar as the Mohammaden and Hindu, meeting and mingling together." In 1193 Qutbuddin Aibak, the slave general of Muhammad Ghori, stormed the Lalkot citadel of the Chauhan king Prithvi Raj III and established the Delhi Sultanate.

Quwwat-ul-Islam Mosque The first task of the new ruler was to clear the ground of the structures of the infidels, their palaces and temples, and to build anew. For this purpose all buildings in Lalkot and Qila Rai Pithora were demolished and the temples razed to the ground. Stone pillars from the debris of these destroyed structures were picked up and re-assembled to form the corridors of the Quwwat-ul-Islam (the might of Islam) mosque.

The site of the ancient Vishnu temple became the site of the first mosque of the Delhi

Opposite page, Above: Old Fort. Below: Ramparts of Lalkot, Mehrauli.

10

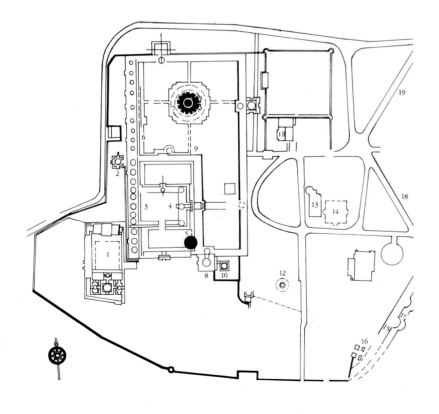

QUTB COMPLEX

To mehrauli
1 *Ala-ud-din's Tomb and College*
2 *Iltumish's Tomb*
3 *Iron Pillar*
4 *Quwwat-ul-Islam Mosque*
5 *Qutb Minar*
6 *Ala-ud-Din-Khilji's Extension*
7 *Alai-Minar*
8 *Alai Darwaza*
9 *Iltumish's Extension*
10 *Imam Zamin's Tomb*
11 *Mughal Mosque*
12 *Major Smith's Cupola*
13 *P.W.D. Rest House*
14 *Garbgaj*
15 *Ramparts of Lalkot*
16 *Chaumukha Gate*
17 *Moat*
18 *To Badarpur*
19 *To Delhi*

Sultanate. The carvings on the pillars, of flowers and vase motifs, bells, and human figures were excellent but in the traditional Hindu style. It outraged the followers of Islam. The figures were mutilated but the effect lingered. To cover this row of pillars a giant screen of arches was built in 1199. It was a magnificent screen with stunning carvings of calligraphic and floral designs. But the Ogee (S-shape) of the arches struck an un-Islamic note. It was a grand architectural achievement and it was left to the succeeding Sultans to rectify these un-Islamic features in the buildings they were to raise around the Qutb. The Quwwat-ul-Islam mosque was the first and a remarkable piece of architecture where the Hindu and Islamic architectural styles were combined to create an hitherto unattempted enterprise.

A relic of the glorious ancient past–the Iron Pillar stands in the centre of the mosque courtyard. Weighing over 6 tonnes, this metallurgical marvel of the Gupta Age (4-5th century) has remained unrusted for centuries. Tradition has it that you are extremely lucky if you can engirdle the shaft with your back towards it.

Qutb Minar In the same year (1199), Aibak ordered the construction of the Qutb Minar, the tower was meant to proclaim to the world the power of Islam. Aibak could complete only the first storey of the tower when he died and his son-in-law and successor, Iltutmish, built the other three storeys of the Minar.

This 238-feet-high tower has four storeys. The first is star-shaped with wedge-shaped flanges alternating with rounded flutings; the second has circular projections; and the third is star-shaped; the fourth and later the fifth as well are circular in white marble originally crowned with a stone kiosk. This red sandstone tower is among the most spectacular sights of the medieval world.

The Quranic verses calligraphed on the surface are done in the most consummate style in Naskh and Kufik characters. But the projected balconies on the tapering exterior are extremely impressive. The stalactite treatment (honeycombing) came from the Egyptian 'gorge' which is an ornamental cornice of roll and hollow mouldings, crowning massive blank walls. It is fantastic in effect, but is in reality based on "correct geometric principles applied to a succession of blind arches, placed in rows one above the other on their periphery," Percy Brown, a historian, explains. The Hindu artisans working on a purely foreign design did a remarkable job establishing their splendid mastery of stone work and surface ornamentation. The Qutb Minar still remains "the most remarkable architectural monument ever produced" in Delhi far surpassing any other structure of this kind in the Islamic world.

In 1368, the Qutb Minar was struck by lightning, damaging the fourth storey. Firoz Tughlaq repaired this and in the process added a fifth storey to Iltutmish's four. In 1503, Sikander Lodi had to make substantial repairs to the tower following severe damage caused by an earthquake. In 1803, the old cupola of the Qutb collapsed, due again to an earthquake. Major Robert Smith carried out extensive repairs and was so swept away by his enthusiasm that he added a cupola of his own design. It was so incongruous with the Qutb architecture that Lord Hardinge had it pulled down in 1848. It is now kept in the Qutb lawns. Also, the restoration by Major Smith on the Kanjuras at the entrance was incorrect in its wrong placement of the inscriptional panel. In general, Smith was criticized for his "Strawberry Hill Gothic" style, which did not go well with the Qutb.

The Qutb Minar has 379 steps and the total height at present is 238 feet and one inch. The early chroniclers called it Minar, but later it came to be called Qutb Minar, perhaps first during the British restoration work at the Qutb, since they identified monuments with their builders. But it is also possible that the Minar was so named after Qutbuddin Bakhtiyar Kaki, a great saint and mentor of Iltutmish, who lived at Mehrauli. The Qutb Minar remains the crowning glory of the architecture of the Delhi Sultanate.

The Qutb means an axis or pole. In this sense it stands like the triumphal standard on the eastern limits of the Islamic world. Surely it was too high to have been used for the muezzin's *azan,* the calling of the faithful to prayer.

Extension of the Mosque Iltutmish, the second Sultan of the Slave Dynasty, doubled the area of the Quwwat-ul-Islam mosque including the Minar within its enclosure and also corrected the Ogee shape in the new arches he built. The ornamentation on the arches was stripped of its dominant floral motifs and replaced with arabesque and geometrical patterns in the Islamic style.

Opposite Page, Top: Pillars of the Vishnu Temple behind the arches of the Quwwat-ul-Islam Mosque at the Quth Minar, Delhi. Above: Balban's tomb near the Quth Minar, noted for its first use of the true arch.

13

Sultan Garhi The cenotaph chamber lies in a pit covered by a flat roof. High walls and strong bastions lend this tomb, called Sultan Gari, a fortified look, grim and forlorn. It is situated a few miles away from the Qutb Minar, but the small single-chamber tomb of Iltutmish stands behind the mosque.

Tomb of Iltutmish It has the most lavishly ornamented interior with Quranic inscriptions in Kufik, Nastalik and Tughra characters. Also noteworthy is the discreet use of white marble on the *mihrab*. The dome on the squinches was possibly never made or gave way too soon. This is yet another example of native artisans creating sculptured effects on the early structures of the Sultanate. The crypt lies in the basement, which is closed to visitors.

Alai Darwaza The Qutb continued to receive additions from the Khiljis (1290-1320), who had succeeded Aibak. Alauddin dreamt of world conquest and intended doubling the area of the great mosque. But the new arches never rose beyond the core masonry of five or six feet. Of the four grand gateways only the southern, the Alai Darwaza (1311), could be completed within his lifetime. The Alai Darwaza is the most splendid example of polychromatic ornamentation using white marble with red sandstone. The pointed arches have spearhead fringes, performed screen windows framed within rectangular bands of calligraphic panels. But the main achievement is the dome on squinches, the first of its kind in Delhi.

To the north of the Qutb stands the 87 feet high rubble core of Alai Minar which Alauddin Khilji had intended to dwarf the Qutb. Only the first storey could be built before the Sultan died.

Tughlaqabad The architectural style at the Qutb retained many traits of the Hindu traditions. When the Tughlaqs came to power a deliberate change was introduced. Structures were purged of their Hindu ornamentation and a grim and military look of buttressed walls appeared as characteristic of the new style.

Ghiyasuddin Tughlaq started building a grand new fort a few kilometers south of the Qutb. Within four years of his rule, during 1320-24, the grand fort of Tughlaqabad was ready with gigantic towers and bastions over massive fortifications. It is surprising how such ponderous stones were lifted to such high positions on walls, since there were no cranes to help. Within the walls of the fort stood grand palaces, basement chambers, mosques, towers, tanks and secret vaults where vast quantities of gold were kept. Tughlaqabad fort was awe-inspiring in its rugged and savage splendour.

Ghiyasuddin had incurred the wrath of the saint Nizamuddin, who cursed the Sultan's city. *"Ya rahe usar, ya base gujjar"* (either it be deserted or else be peopled by the Gujjar tribesmen) because Ghiyasuddin had created great difficulties for the saint who was building his *baoli*. When the vanity of the Sultan made him furious at the saint's lack of fear, he warned the saint of serious consequences when he returned from his Bengal campaign. Nizamuddin quipped *"Hunuz Dilli dur ast"* (Delhi is yet far away). When the Sultan approached Delhi,

Right: Ornamentation on the tomb of Iltutmish, near Qutb Minar Opposite page: Above: The Qutb balconies, spectacular stalactite work. Below left: Corridor of the Quwwat-ul-Islam Mosque at the Qutb Minar. Right: Visitors trying to gather the Iron Pillar at the Qutb Minar.

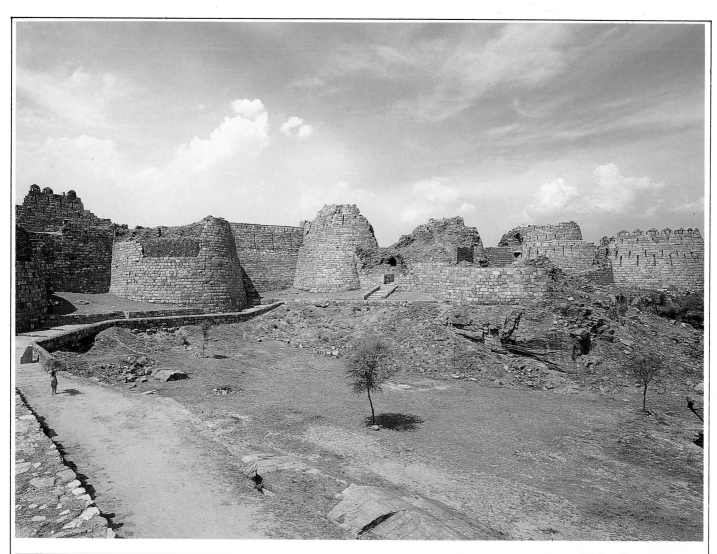

his son Muhammad arranged a reception for him under a grandiose wooden canopy. The saluting elephants stepped over the contraption causing the canopy to collapse on the Sultan, killing him instantly. The Sultan, as the saint had hinted, never reached Delhi and Tughlaqabad was abandoned soon after

Tomb of Ghiyasuddin Tughlaq During his lifetime, Ghiyasuddin Tughlaq built his mausoleum in a small fortress opposite the fort, surrounded by an artificial lake. The mausoleum is an irregular pentagon in plan, with an impressive battlemented wall for defence during an emergency. The magnificent tomb has buttressed walls and discreet ornamentation with white marble on red sandstone. Of some beauty is the lotus fringe on the arched entrance. The pointed Tartar dome in marble, crowned by a lotus and melon motif, looks majestic. Fergusson, a historian of Indian architecture, says of the tomb: "The sloping walls and almost Egyptian solidity of this mausoleum, combined with the bold and massive towers of the fortifications that surrounded it, form a model of a warrior's tomb hardly to be rivalled anywhere...."

Adilabad Muhammad Tughlaq, soon after coming to the throne, started work on his fort at Adilabad, adjacent to Tughlaqabad. One of his characteristically ambitious plans was to enclose, within a walled area, the population which lay scattered in Mehrauli, Tughlaqabad Kilokhiri and Siri. He called it Jahanpanah, but abandoned the project for want of funds, which he had squandered in shifting the capital to Devagiri in the Deccan and then moving back to Delhi. Muhammad Tughlaq was buried in the tomb of his parents at Tughlaqabad.

Firoz Shah Kotla Firoz Tughlaq (1351-88), was extremely fond of building on a grand scale, but he was also aware of the need for maintaining the existing Delhi monuments and repaired most of them. He realized that the water supply was a major reason why these cities south of Delhi had to be abandoned, but solved this problem by building his new fortress near the river Yamuna. Firoz Shah's Kotla was a grand citadel with some magnificent palaces, long, winding corridors, and a *baoli* (stepped well). Kotla also contained two other magnificent structures which were the pride of the city.

The Jama Masjid could accommodate ten thousand men at prayer and had a central pillar on which were inscribed the achievements of Firoz Tughlaq. This mosque was completely destroyed by Timur, who removed the building material for a mosque in Samarkand. The pyramidal structure crowned by an Ashokan Pillar, a monolithic tapering column, dated 3rd century B.C. brought as a trophy of victory from Topra near Ambala, was an object of mystery to his contemporaries who failed to decipher the inscriptions. James Princep finally unravelled the script in 1837. The polish on the pillar still remains brilliant and smooth. Firoz Tughlaq's city stretched between the Ridge and Mehrauli and contained schools, caravanserais, hospitals and mosques.

Mosques However, for us the greatest gift Firoz Tughlaq gave to the city of Delhi was the large number of mosques he built – austere, high-plinthed, like frowning fortresses. Among these are the Kali Masjids at Turkman Gate and Nizamuddin, Khirki Masjid at Sheikh Serai and the Begampuri Masjid near Badi Manzil in Jahanpanah. These mosques are grand and spacious, with tapering buttresses at the four corners, multi-domed roofs and arch and beam entrances.

Khirki Masjid is particularly beautiful as the courtyard is covered and only four openings are provided for light in the interior. The 85 small domes on top add a novel feature in architecture. Begampuri Masjid is known for its huge courtyard surrounded by arcaded cloisters. The pylon is high and magnificent.

Khan-i-Jahan Tilangani, the Prime Minister of Firoz Shah Tughlaq who had built most of these mosques, made yet another bold architectural experiment in designing an octagonal tomb for himself. The cenotaph chamber is surrounded by a verandah, heavy broad eaves provide shade and shelter from rain and cupolas on the roof add grandeur to the structure. Built near Nizamuddin, this is now in ruins, but it became a prototype for the royal tombs of the Sayyad and Lodi kings who followed the Tughlaqs.

Tomb at Lodi Gardens The tombs of the Sayyad and Lodi kings (1414-1526) stand in Lodi Gardens. The Sayyads inherited a depleted kingdom and stayed at the Kotla. They only built tombs in open gardens in marked contrast to the closed-in tombs of the Tughlaqs. The octagonal tomb of Muhammad Shah (1450), the third ruler of the Sayyad dynasty, has sloping

Opposite page, Top: Tughlaqabad Fort. Left: Tomb of Ghiyasuddin Tughlaq. Far left: Ruins of the Jama Masjid at Firoz Shah Kotla, Delhi.

buttresses, projecting eaves and a lotus-topped dome and was a model for many octagonal tombs in the following years. It is located in the open garden and is beautifully landscaped.

Nearby in a walled enclosure, stands the tomb of Sikander Lodi (1517-18), noted for its first use of the "double dome". This Persian concept of a "double dome" was perfected in the great Mughal tombs of Humayun in Delhi and of Mumtaz Mahal in Agra.

The square tombs – a single square cenotaph chamber with a high dome – were meant for ministers and nobles. The straight lines of the exterior wall are broken into facades suggesting a double or triple storey structure. In fact, there is always a single storey within.

Bada Gumbad and Shish Gumbad in the Lodi Gardens are two splendid examples of the typical Lodi style square tomb. Decorations in blue tiles, use of heavy brackets and a painted ceiling – characteristics of square tombs – are used to great advantage in these tombs.

The Bada Gumbad Masjid (1404), carries the most excellent ornamentation in stucco. The exquisite filigree work and decorative calligraphic bands on arches and medallions make it the most beautiful mosque of its kind in India, though architecturally it has no striking feature.

The Delhi Sultanate gradually came to decline under the Lodis but they had absorbed the best qualities of Hindu architecture – its strength and grace. Native artisans had mastered the principles of Islamic architecture and combined the best of both the styles to create splendid surface decorations. The Hindu style never really disappeared entirely. It discreetly took a back seat, surfacing again when the occasion permitted. Indo-Islamic architecture is thus a fusion of both the divergent styles.

Purana Qila Despite the lack of any structural evidence to support the popular belief that the Purana Qila is the site of the legendary Indraprastha, the fort continues to enjoy a reputation. The present structures were built by Humayun and Sher Shah. Humayun constructed the massive walls and three gateways before he lost his kingdom to Sher Shah. Dinpanah, Humayun's city, was as ill-fated as its builder. The northern Tallaqi Darwaza is closed to viewers. The southern gateway opening towards the zoo is also closed. The western gateway provides entrance to the vast area, within which there are only two structures built by Sher Shah.

The Qila-Kuhna mosque (1541), is a grand structure with a five-arched facade. This has the strength of the massive and ornamental Afghan style. This mosque has the most splendid *mehrab* in white marble. The central arch carries splendid decoration in white and coloured marble, which looks gorgeous against the background of red sandstone. The narrow fluted pilasters flanking the central arch are an experiment leading to the erection of minars as part of mosque architecture under the Mughals.

Sher Mandal Sher Mandal is a small octagonal tower in red sandstone, a double storeyed structure crowned with a pavilion. Humayun later used it as his library and fell from its steps as his foot caught in his dress when he knelt in prayer. He died within three days of this accident.

There is also a deep *baoli* near Sher Mandal which still supplies water to the gardens. Excavations at the Purana Qila yielded no evidence of the Mahabharat era, thought it exposed to view stratified levels showing continued occupation of this site from the Mauryan period to the Mughals.

The river which used to flow below the Purana Qila has long since changed its course and the moat on the other three sides is a mere dry ditch. Lal Darwaza, one of the grand gateways built by Sher Shah, stands at a little distance opposite the western gateway. It is the only structure which was part of Shergarh, Sher Shah's city.

Humayun's Tomb Humayun died in 1556 and Haji Begum, his widow, built the mausoleum for him in 1569. The 300 Arab craftsmen she brought with her are responsible for the pronounced Persian features of this magnificent garden tomb. Mirak Mirza Ghiyas, who designed the tomb, presented the first perfect example of a double dome with the inner shell forming the ceiling over the cenotaph and the outer creating the effect of a grand height. The mausoleum is built on a platform four feet in height. On this stands the raised plinth 22 feet high. This, in fact, provides the basement, consisting of interconnected rooms, with a 17-arched facade on each side. On this second platform stands the octagonal structure

of the tomb in red sandstone, discreetly ornamented with white marble panes. The high bulbous dome rises over 38 metres (125 feet). The four arches on each side are 12.2 metres in height (40 feet), flanked by smaller arches and recessed windows closed with lattice screens.

The cenotaph chamber contains the grave of Humayun under a cool vaulted ceiling. North-east of her husband's grave lies Haji Begum in an octagonal small room.

The platform provided space for many ill-fated princes of the Mughal dynasty, notably the headless body of Dara Shikoh, Shahjahan's crown prince, Jehandar Shah, Farrukhsiyar, Rafi-ud-darajat, Rafi-ud-daula and Alamgir II. It was at Humayun's tomb that the last Mughal Emperor, Bahadur Shah II, sought refuge from the British in 1857 and was captured. Also captured here were Bahadur Shah's three princes, who were shot dead near the Khooni Darwaza.

The garden at this tomb has been laid out in the Persian style of a Chahr Bagh, with paved stone avenues and narrow water channels. It is still maintained in its orinigal grandeur. Humayun's tomb and its gardens later inspired Shahjahan to work out a model for the Taj Mahal, bringing the Persian concept of a garden tomb to its most perfect culmination.

In the neighbourhood stands Nila Gumbad covered with blue tiles and an exquisitely painted ceiling. Also to be found are Babur's tomb (within the enclosure), Isa Khan's octagonal tomb and a mosque, and Afsarwala tomb and mosque (1556-67).

Aran ki Serai and Bu Halima's Garden These are the ruins of Arab ki Serai where the Arabian craftsmen were housed by Haji Begum. The tall gateway to this Serai is still very impressive. Bu Halima's garden tomb predates Humayun's tomb and the identity of the lady buried here is still a subject for research. Humayun's tomb stands at the centre of Shahjahanabad and the southern area of Delhi.

Tomb of Abdul Rahim Khan-i-Khana This central area of Delhi has two more tombs of immense beauty. Near Nizamuddin stands the grand mausoleum of Abdul Rahim Khan-i-Khana, Akbar's counsellor (c. 1625). Built on a high platform, it is single-chamber, high-domed structure which also served as a model for the Taj Mahal. The marble facing of the structure was removed for building the Safdarjung mausoleum at some distance from Humayun's tomb.

Tomb of Nizamuddin Nearby, in a congested locality across the road, stands the small tomb of Nizamuddin Auliya, the most venerated saint of his times, who lived through the rule of many Sultans of Delhi (1235-1325). The saint's defiance of Ghiyasuddin Tughlaq is still remembered. The original modest grave was remodelled in 1562 by a noble and further royal devotion to the saint's memory inspired decoration of the canopy in mother-of-pearl and marble lattice screens executed in the most flawless designs.

Tomb of Amir Khusro Amir Khusro, the saint's chief disciple, also lies buried near his mentor. As if seeking the saint's blessings, a few royal personages sought burial here. Jahanara, the eldest daughter of Shahjahan, lies in an open grave with the inscription: "Let nought cover my grave save the green grass. For grass suffices as the covering of the body." It was her gesture of humility.

Tomb of Muhammad Shah Muhammad Shah II, during whose rule Nadir Shah plundered Delhi, died in 1748 and is buried here. Also buried here is Jehangir II, eldest son of Akbar II.

Tomb of Atagha Khan and Chausath Khambha Two other tombs in the neighbourhood deserve mention: Atagha Khan's small square tomb with gorgeous polychromatic decoration in *pietra dura* and Chausath Khambha (1625) a marble hall with excellent latticed screens. The great Urdu poet Mirza Ghalib is also buried here in a modest marble pavilion.

Nizamuddin *baoli* lies on the north-west corner of the tomb enclosure. It was during the construction of this *baoli* that the saint was irritated by Ghiyasuddin Tughlaq's haughty command forbidding workers to work at the site.

Many kings and emperors have come and gone, remembered for a while and then consigned to oblivion and books of history. The memory of saints enlightens our days long after they are gone. Nizamuddin's tomb is frequented everyday by hundreds of devotees, both Hindus and Muslims.

Opposite page, top: Tomb of Nizamuddin, near Humayun's Tomb, New Delhi. Right: Tomb of Safdarjung, New Delhi. Far right: The humility of a Mughal princess – tomb of Jahanara Begum at Nizamuddin.

लाहौर द्वार
LAHORE GATE

Left: The Red Fort, Shahjahanabad, Delhi. Top: Painted ceiling of the Diwan-i-Khas, Red Fort, Delhi. Above: 'Nashiman zilli-i-Ilahi' (seat of the shadow of God), the royal seat at Diwan-i-Aam, Red Fort, Delhi.

Safdarjung's Tomb Safdarjung's Tomb is the last of the great garden tombs in Delhi. Like its predecessors, this mausoleum is built on a raised platform. The red and buff coloured stone of the structure has been ornamented with white marble and the high bulbous dome site guarded by four corner polygonal towers. Built for Nawab Safdarjung of Oudh (1753), this mausoleum has a beautiful Mughal garden as at Humayun's Tomb, which it imitates in style and setting.

The Safdarjung mausoleum was the last grand edifice built towards the end of the Mughal rule, and marks the decline of a great architectural tradition born of Hindu and Islamic styles.

Red Fort Qala-i-Mubarak (the fortunate citadel) was the centre of Shahjahanabad, the capital of the Mughal empire after 1648. It took nine years to complete this great and massive fort, designed by Ustad Ahmad Lahori and two other architects, Ustad Hamid and Ustad Hira. Shahjahan entered his new fort on an auspicious day and the fort was called Qala-i-Mualla (the exalted fort). But, due to its red sandstone structure, it was generally called Lal Qila or Red Fort.

Visitors enter the fort through the Lahore Gate, which has a high central arch flanked by subsidiary structures. The barbican in front of this gate was Aurangzeb's addition, who thought that since the city's main street lay in a straight line facing the royal throne in the Diwani-i-Aam, people had to dismount to pay respect to the seat and suffer inconvenience. Beyond the Lahore Gate stands Chatta Chowk, a vaulted arcade with a Gothic arch and an octagonal open space in the centre. This is the market of the fort, where merchants from distant lands assembled for displaying their work. Today it is a market for souvenirs and fake antiques.

The road leads to Naqqar Khana, where music was played at regular hours and the residential palaces lie beyond this beautifully sculptured double storeyed gateway. Between Chatta Chowk and Zaqqar Khana lay a tank and some arcaded quarters, now removed.

Diwan-i-Aam The Diwan-i-Aam, the hall of public audience, is a colonnaded structure in red sandstone. The superbly sculptured engrailed arches on pillars were in their heyday coated with a white plaster. The royal seat is a canopy inlaid with the most splendid *pietra dura* work on marble. The craftsmanship of marble panels depicting Orpheus and some exotic birds is the work of Austin of Bordeaux. These panels were removed to the Victoria and Albert Museum in London and Lord Curzon had them returned and restored to their original place. It is the most magnificent canopy with a Bengali roof. When the Mughal emperor sat in audience, the spectacle had incredible grandeur: magnificent carpets, fabulous tapestries, and brocaded canopies, railings in gold and silver and a host of nobles and dignitaries standing with bowed heads in front of His Majesty. The Vizier stood on the

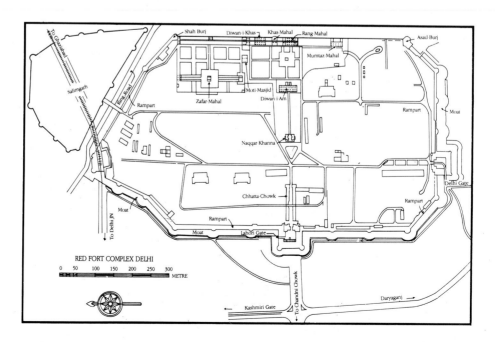

Opposite page: The lotus-shaped marble fountain in the Rang Mahal, Red Fort, Delhi. Following page: Jama Masjid, Delhi.

24

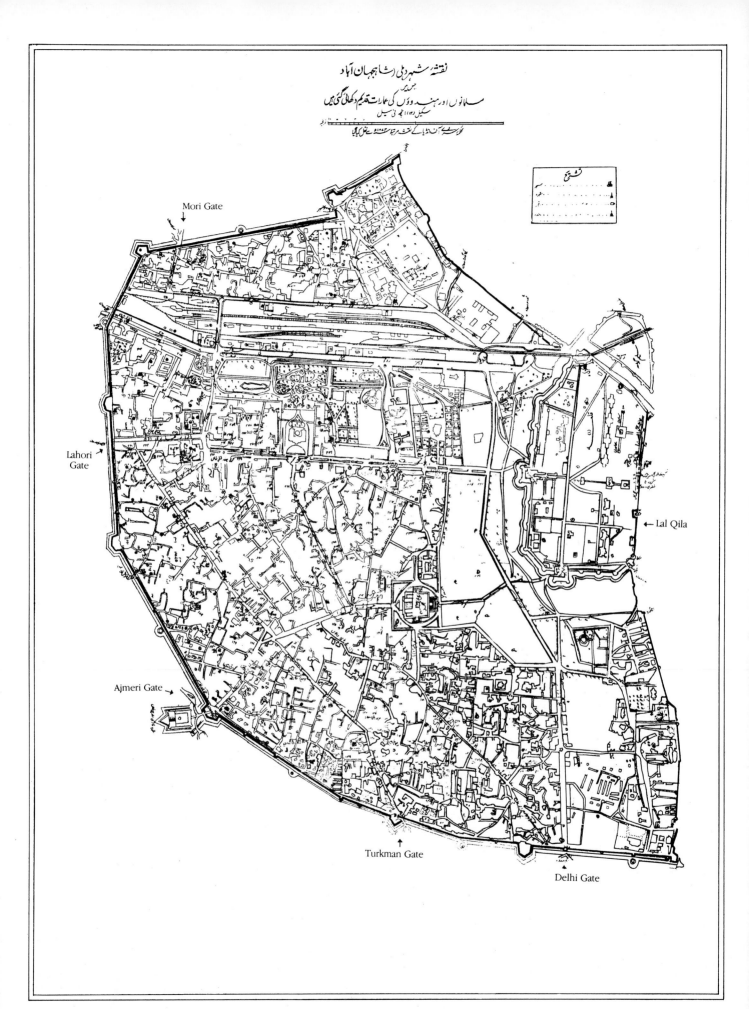

نقشہ شہر دہلی (شاہجہان آباد)
جس میں
مسلمانوں اور ہندوؤں کی عمارات قدیم دکھائی گئی ہیں

Mori Gate

Lahori
Gate

Ajmeri Gate

Turkman Gate

Delhi Gate

Lal Qila

28

marble platform below the royal canopy. Petitions were heard and judgements pronounced on the spot for immediate execution. Processions of animals and soldiers marched past in a scene of unparalleled splendour.

Rang Mahal Behind the Diwan-i-Aam lie three palaces made of marble on the river front. The Rang Mahal was meant for the royal seraglio with windows covered with lattice screens. The exquisite marble lotus fountain carved out of a single block of a marble is the *piece de resistance*. It was part of the water channels running through all the palaces. The silver ceiling was removed by Farrukhsiyar, replaced by another one in copper which was also removed and replaced by the present one in wood.

Mumtaz Mahal now houses the musuem. It was also part of the *zenana* quarters. A grand garden with fountains lying between the Diwan-i-Aam and Rang Mahal was destroyed by the British, but has now been partly restored. A huge marble basin restored to its place on the raised platform gives a faint idea of the original grandeur of this garden. The palaces towards the south-east corner have all been destroyed completely, surviving only in books of history. Only the small Asad Burj stands in an unfrequented corner.

Khas Mahal was really the royal residence and contains a marble screen with the most exquisitely worked floral patterns. The 'Scale of Justice' is carved on the upper section of this screen.

Diwan-i-Khas Diwan-i-Khas was the hall of private audience and built entirely of marble columns inlaid with precious stones. The original silver ceiling was removed by the Marathas. This was the most gorgeously decorated palace in the fort and stood within an enclosure marked by rows of arcaded rooms where a *lal purdah* (red curtain) separated it from the rest of the fort. Entrance was for a few, extremely privileged people.

Magnificent carpets from Herat, colourful awnings, bolsters, cushions and tapestries were spread all over. On a grand marble dais stood the legendary Peacock Throne, built of solid gold railings encrusted with the costliest and most exquisite gems, pearls, rubies and sapphires. In fact, the treasures of the great Mughals were closely searched to find the most exquisite stones which were used for ornamenting this throne. Bebadal Khan had designed the Peacock Throne as a masterpiece of craftsmanship. Frequently hailed as the world's most gorgeous throne, it was valued at £12,037,500 by Tavernier, a contemporary traveller. When the Emperor wore the Kohinoor and sat on this throne it was a scene of splendour unparalleled perhaps in the history of the world. The famous Persian inscription: "If there is a Paradise on the face of the earth, it is this, it is this", summed up the grandeur of the Diwan-i-Khas. The Nihir-i-Bihisht flowed through the channels to add its own charm to the hall.

The Diwan-i-Khas, with the decline of Mughal power, witnessed the successive puppet kings insulted and tortured under the inscription. In 1739, Nadir Shah took away with him to Persia the Peacock Throne and the Kohinoor. Others removed the ceiling and inlaid stones. Only a shell of the former structure has been left behind.

Further north stands the Shah Burj, where the Emperor sat for extremely confidential consultations with princes and ministers. It has a mirror encrusted hall, the Sheesh Mahal. The gardens – Mahtab Bagh and Hayat Baksh – stood here with the grand channels of water running through the flowering trees. The two marble pavilions, Sawan and Bhadon, have survived the ravages of the British occupation of the fort after 1857.

Moti Masjid Moti Masjid, a small marble mosque, was built by Aurangzeb in 1662. The original copper on the door was removed at some point. For its exquisitely carved ornamentation on the engrailed arches, Moti Masjid is still regarded as a gem of Mughal architecture.

Despite the large-scale demolition of the smaller structures in the fort, particularly the arcaded galleries, residential areas and gardens, the Red Fort still contains some palaces which even in their present state stand as evidence of the legendary Mughal splendour.

Jama Masjid Facing the Red Fort stands the Jama Masjid (1650) in red sandstone. India's largest mosque, it commands the densely populated area of Shahjahanabad. This mosque is the pride of Mughal architecture. It is a simple but grand structure with three large gateways providing entry to a huge courtyard paved with stones. Pillared cloisters surround the open courtyard. The central *Iwan* is flanked by two slender minarets in red sandstone striped with white marble which are 130 feet in height and crowned by elegant cupolas. The three marble domes are also ornamented with streaks of black marble. These bulbous domes contribute a

Opposite Page: Reproduction of an old map of the walled city of Delhi.

remarkable grandeur to the majestic simplicity of the mosque. The *mihrab* and the *mimbar* (arch and pulpit) are in unornamented white marble. In the north eastern corner of the courtyard is a tiny mosque housing the sacred relics of Hazrat Mohammad, which Shahjahan inherited from Amir Timur. Since Shahjahan's days, the mosque has been the centre of the walled city.

Francois Bernier, the French visitor to the Mughal court in 1663, described the magnificence of Shahjahan's procession going to the Jama Masjid: "The king leaves the fortress, sometimes on an elephant, decorated with rich trappings, and a canopy supported by painted and gilt pillars; and sometimes in a throne of gleaming with azure and gold, placed on a litter covered with scarlet or brocade, which eight chosen men, in handsome attire, carry on their shoulders. A body of *Omrahs* follow the king, some on horse back, and others in *Palkeys*; and among the *Omrahs* are seen a great number of *Mansebdars*, and the bearers of silver mace... I cannot say that this train resembles the pompous processions, or (which is a more appropriate term) the masqueraders of the Grand *Seignier*, or the martial retinues of European Monarchs: its magnificence is of a different character; but is is not therefore the less royal."

The Emperor and his entourage have been replaced by the common man of today and the Jama Masjid is visited by thousands each Friday.

New Delhi On December 12, 1911, at the Royal Darbar in Delhi, King George V announced that Delhi was to be the capital of British power in India. This foundation stone, laid at a place north of Delhi, later had to be shifted to Raisina Hill. Two noted architects, Edwin Lutyens and Herbert Baker, designed most of the great buildings of Imperial Delhi. But, from the beginning, the plans of expenditure and design of structures were embroiled in heated controversies and quarrels. Lutyens and Baker ridiculed Indian architecture as onions and turnips set upon stones, grotesque and over-ornamented. For them, the Imperial form of architecture was the solution to this problem. But they were compelled by the general opinion and climate of Delhi to incorporate such striking Indian features as *chajjas* (stone cornices), *jalis* (latticed screens), *chattris* (canopies) and lotus and bell motifs. The large open courtyards were also an unavoidable part of the plans. Grudgingly, they decided to adopt these features. Of course, with the cost of construction escalating every year, many grandiose plans had to be abandoned.

The Viceroy's House (Rashtrapati Bhawan) was the showpiece of Lutyens' work, a grand palace larger than Versailles in red and cream coloured sandstone combining features of "a giant Indian bungalow, embattled Rajput fortress and Mughal tomb." With the amenities of a English country house, with ground halls, 300 rooms and royal galleries, courtyards and gardens, this palace dominates the ground with its portico comprising severel columns topped by the dome in copper and a Sanchi style stone railing. In the central courtyard stands the Jaipur Column, a gift of Madho Singh II, the Maharaja of Jaipur. With a remarkable bronze lotus from which emerges a crystal star on top, this 145 feet high column became the symbol of British power in India. An exquisitely laid out Mughal Garden, complete with fountain channels, a butterfly garden and a circular pool at the northern extremity of the Viceroy's House are part of the complex. It is open to the public in February and March every year.

The two Secretariat blocks which have pushed the Viceroy's Palace to the background, were designed by Baker. There are high-ceilinged rooms, grand winding staircases, and corridors and minor courtyards in addition to the Indian features. An inscription was rather prophetic: "Liberty will not descend to a people; a people must raise themselves to liberty; it is a blessing which must be earned before it is enjoyed." The people of India earned this freedom from the builders of Imperial Delhi in 1947, sixteen years after the completion of New Delhi.

Parliament House, Baker's creation, is a set of three semi-circular halls girdled by a most handsome colonnade of 144 pillars. Its dome is rather low, concealed behind the attic floor added in 1929. But the structure is grand and unique in concept.

Lutyens had designed the Grand Plaza (Vijay Chowk) with its majestic shallow fountains with obelisk. The War Memorial Arch (India Gate), stands at the other end of this great axis. The 139 feet arch records the names of 60,000 soldiers who died in World War I, and 13,516 who were missing and feared dead. Today an eternal flame burns here in honour of the Amar Jawan, a homage to the bravery of Indian soldiers. The canopy, set within a small pool

Top: Rashtrapati Bhawan (President's House). New Delhi. Above: Portrait of Edwin Lutyens, who designed most of the buildings of imperial Delhi and the rough sketches of the North and South Blocks including Reshtrapati Bhawan. Left: Parliament House (Sansad Bhawan), New Delhi. Following page: Bird's-eye view of Connaught Place, New Delhi.

once had the marble statue of King George V, now removed to the Statue Park at the site of the Darbar of 1911. New Delhi was formally inaugurated by the Viceroy, Lord Irwin, on February 9, 1931.

The plans for many grand buildings on both sides of the King's Way (Raj Path) had to be abandoned and only the National Archives could be completed by Lutyens. Two other architects, who have been unjustly ignored, were Robert Tor Russell who designed Connaught Place, the Commander-in-Chief's House (Teen Murti House), Eastern and Western Courts and a great number of bungalows and government buildings and Henry Medd who designed the two beautiful Churches – the Cathedral Church of the Redemption (1935) near North Avenue and the Sacred Heart Church (1931) near the Circular General Post Office (Gole Dakhana). The National Stadium was designed by Russell, but Lutyens had initially disapproved of the idea. However, it was built in place of a large artificial lake where the grand axis of the King's Way was to terminate in the shadows of Purana Qila reflected in the water.

The British did exactly what the Turkish Sultans of the Delhi Sultanate did in 1193. Both hated traditional Indian architecture but had to incorporate its features in their own architecture. New Delhi buildings certainly look imperial but a little out of place in free India.

Jantar Mantar On Parliament Street stands Jantar Mantar, the first of Sawai Jai Singh II's five centres of astronomical studies. Built in 1724, this is the only structure of some beauty belonging to the rule of Muhammad Shah II in Delhi. The Jantar Mantar at Jaipur, however, is bigger and more spectacular than the one in Delhi.

Birla Mandir With the building of New Delhi, the last in the chain of cities built on this glorious ground, the grand Indo-Islamic architectural tradition seems to have declined, more so with the mushrooming of skyscrapers in Lutyens' New Delhi. Still, two comparatively new structures, both temples, are of some importance and beauty. The Lakshmi Narayan Temple, better known as Birla Mandir after its builder, Raja Baldev Rai Birla, was built in 1938. It is a complex of shrines and ornamental gardens. Surprisingly, this is the first Hindu temple built on such a grand scale since the fall of Prithvi Raj Chauhan in 1192.

The other is the Baha'i Temple in south Delhi. This lotus-shaped structure is fashioned out of white Italian marble. The marvellous lotus, symbol of purity and perfection is designed to function as a series of skylights, with glazing provided at the apex of the inner petals, the internal vertical surface of the outer petals and the external side of the entrance. Its nine sides represent nine religions flourishing in various parts of the world, thus rendering it into a synthesis of the diverse religions. Enter into its grand hall to meditate in silence.

Right: Jantar Mantar, New Delhi. Opposite page: Top: Baha'i Temple, New Delhi. Below: India Gate, New Delhi.

34

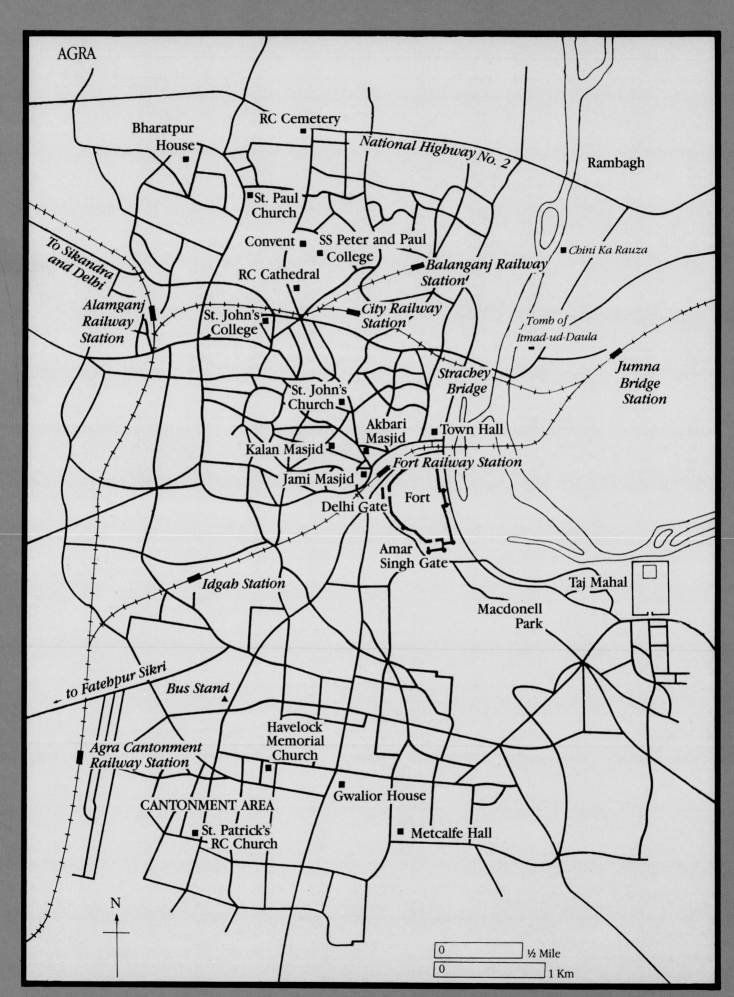

AGRA

Bharatpur
House

RC Cemetery

National Highway No. 2

Rambagh

St. Paul
Church

Convent

SS Peter and Paul
College

Chini Ka Rauza

RC Cathedral

*Balanganj Railway
Station'*

*To Sikandra
and Delhi*

*Alamganj
Railway
Station*

St. John's
College

*City Railway
Station'*

*Tomb of
Itmad-ud-Daula*

St. John's
Church

*Strachey
Bridge*

*Jumna
Bridge
Station*

Akbari
Masjid

Town Hall

Kalan Masjid

Fort Railway Station

Jami Masjid

Delhi Gate

Fort

Idgah Station

Amar
Singh Gate

Taj Mahal

Macdonell
Park

to Fatehpur Sikri

Bus Stand

Havelock
Memorial
Church

*Agra Cantonment
Railway Station*

Gwalior House

CANTONMENT AREA

St. Patrick's
RC Church

Metcalfe Hall

N

| 0 | ½ Mile |
| 0 | 1 Km |

Agra

The First Mughal City

Agra is only 223 km (139 miles) from Delhi and can be reached in four hours of comfortable driving. The history of the city is not very ancient. In fact, in the *Mahabharata*, it is referred to as a deeply forested area, peopled by tribes. Later, when it became a town, it was only an insignificant adjunct to the Rajput kingdoms. It is only in the fifteenth and sixteenth centuries that Agra emerged as an important city, where the Lodis built a fort. Delhi was close by and rulers moved conveniently between the two cities.

In 1502, Sikander Lodi of the Afghan dynasty chose Agra as his capital. A few tombs of the Lodi era can still be seen near Sikandra. Babur defeated Ibrahim Lodi in 1526 to found the Mughal Empire and he sent Humayun to capture the treasure at Agra Fort. Here the family of the Gwalior king sought refuge in a cellar and presented Humayun with the Kohinoor, the biggest diamond in the world, seeking a promise of security for themselves. The Raja had died with Ibrahim Lodi on the battlefield. Soon Babur moved in with his forces and Agra became the seat of a new kingdom. Agra remained the capital of the Mughals between 1526 and 1585. Later, Akbar and Jehangir preferred Lahore to Agra and, in 1648, Shahjahan formally abandoned Agra in favour of Delhi, where he had built a new city and fort.

Mughal Emperor Akbar

Agra rose into prominence when the Mughals built new palaces and an impressive fort. It flourished as a trading centre for magnificent Persian carpets, diamonds and precious stones and miraculously woven and embroidered fabrics. Under the Mughals, Agra assuredly had become the most splendid capital of all Asia, tales of its pomp and glory reaching distant lands. It was renamed Akbarabad, after the third and greatest Mughal emperor. The city's caravanserais were always overflowing with people from distant lands. The city had a great number of *hammams* (baths), mosques, schools and markets and grew into a maze of narrow lanes stocked with the most expensive and fabulous goods from all over the world. The swarm of people everywhere became so dense that people could hardly move about freely and the city could not be circumscribed in a day.

This state of prosperity lasted only so long as Agra remained the capital of the Mughal Empire. After 1648, when Shahjahan moved to Delhi and carried with him the Peacock Throne and the Kohinoor, the fortunes of Agra city took a reverse turn, rendering it an undefended hunting ground for the Rohillas, Jats, Marathas and the British. To the world, Agra is remembered as the city of the Taj Mahal, the greatest gift Shahjahan gave to his former capital.

Babur was greatly disappointed with Agra. His Persian taste for well laid out gardens and pavilions were revolted at the sight before him. He decided to build a garden across the river but no site appealed to him as suitable for a terraced garden. *Baburnama* records his repulsion at the lack of water, and the dust and heat of India which oppressed him all the more strikingly. Memories of Kabul and Samarkand made him feel frustrated at his present lot. "One of the great defects of Hindustan," Babur wrote, "being its lack of running waters, it kept coming to my mind that water should be made to flow by means of wheels wherever I might settle down, also that grounds should be laid out in an orderly and symmetrical form."

Aram Bagh With a plan for a garden to suit his requirements, Babur laid the foundation of a Char Bagh, enclosed, private and quadripartite. Presently called Aram Bagh, this was the first of the great Mughal gardens in India. A number of terraces, pools, pavilions and raised platforms were built in the midst of colourful and fruit bearing trees. This garden was later completed by Humayun and when Jehangir handed it over to his queen, a *baradari* decorated with murals was added to the highest terrace on the river front. The well supplying water to the innumerable streams and fountains was dug at the western corner.

37

Babur's garden looked a copy of his favourite garden in Kabul. It has the splendour of a Persian carpet. Citrus oranges, cypresses and poplars were planted to provide fruits and grapes grew in abundance. Here, amidst a setting of paradise on earth, the first Mughal emperor would sit receiving visitors, deciding state matters, enjoy poetry reading sessions, listen to music or just drink arak, his favourite brew. The river flowed quietly below these terraces as Babur sat below his splendidly decorated pavilions, shaded by gorgeous awnings, lost in thoughts about Kabul and Samarkand.

You can still see the ruins of some structures, wells, water chutes and channels around small octagonal platforms and some terraces. Faint traces of floral murals at Jehangir's *baradari* remind you of its heyday, when royal parties were held here and harem beauties could breathe fresh air and enjoy themselves. But no trace can be found of Zehra Bagh and Dehra Bagh, the two other gardens laid out by Babur. They have been destroyed by time and neglect and the increasing encroachments of a growing population. Babur had called Aram Bagh Gul Afshan, which was later renamed Nur Afshan during Jehangir's reign. Babur was temporarily buried in this garden in 1530 before his body was taken to his Bagh-i-Wafa in Kabul for a permanent burial.

The Fort Babur, the founder of the Mughal empire, ruled for only four years, between 1520-30. Except for the construction of some structures near Aram Bagh, he built nothing else and remained busy fighting battles and consolidating his early gains. The lacklustre Humayun had little time to think of building forts in Agra. In fact, he shifted his capital to Delhi, where he built Dinpanah, his own fort and city around Purana Qila. When Akbar succeeded Humayun, he returned to Agra and between 1565-1571 built an impregnable fort on the dilapidated structure of the Lodi fort, sometimes called Badalgarh. The lofty crenellated battlements cast their protective shadow on the far stretching rows of mansions and palaces built on the river bank. The massive towers, bastions and grand gateways guarded the palaces within the fort walls. The red sandstone fort of Akbar soon became the grand citadel of Mughal power, and drawn to it by tales of magnificence, came a host of painters, chroniclers, physicians, philosophers and craftsmen. They were welcomed by Akbar and settled down to make Agra an enviable city.

Today you can see distinctive architectural styles in the fort. The massive, red sandstone structures, trabeate in construction with heavy brackets, ornamented with Hindu motifs typical of Akbar's earlier buildings. The transition from stone to marble began under Jehangir and flourished under Shahjahan. There was an emphasis on marble columns splendidly ornamented with costly stones in colour, engrailed arches, delicate trellised screens and fountains, all displaying the splendour Shahjahan loved.

As you cross the drawbridge and look at the towering height of Amar Singh Gate and the massive towers of the inner gate, in the first grand quadrangle you cannot miss the giant stone cup in front of the Jehangir Mahal. Possibly it was used as a bath by Nur Jahan who filled it with water and rose petals. It is still an object of curiosity and conjecture.

Right: Khas Mahal, built by Shah Jahan, Red Fort, Agra. Opposite page: Aram Bagh, the first Mughal garden in India built by Babur, across the Yamuna river in Agra.

Left: Red Fort, Agra. Top: Diwan-i-Aam, Red Fort, Agra. Above: Jehangir Mahal, Red Fort, Agra.

41

Jehangir Mahal is the first royal palace. Built by Akbar for his wife Jodha Bai, a princess of Amber and mother of Salim, the heir apparent, it is reached through an impressive gateway. The inner courtyard has beautiful halls with profuse carvings on stone, exquisitely carved heavy brackets, piers and cross-beams – a demonstration of the superior craft of the native artisan. Many panels in the eastern hall carry stucco paintings in gold and blue in the Persian style. This is the most impressive of Akbar's palaces surviving at the fort.

The other palaces towards the Shah Burj at the northern corner are now hopeless ruins, visited by the curious and scholars. The Jehangir Mahal facade towards the riverfront is really a verandah with tall graceful columns providing the first view of the Taj from windows on the eastern wall.

Khas Mahal, north of Jehangir Mahal, is a grand palace in white marble in front of Anguri Bagh. It is flanked by beautiful pavilions with the famous Bengali gilded copper roofs used for Jehanara's apartments and in the northern corner stands the Sheesh Mahal, ladies, bath, decorated with myriad pieces of glass and a fountain. Back within the spacious and luxuriant Khas Mahal, cast a look at the windows closed with admirable *jali* work through which the meandering current of the Yamuna and the Taj at the far end presents grand scene. But within the fort. it is the vast courtyard and the garden with its effect of openness which adds a new dimension to the splendour.

Moving north over staircases, through concealed passages and walled interiors you reach Musamman Burj or Jasmine Tower, the most luxuriantly ornamental apartments and viewing gallery, poetically described as "hanging like a fairy bower over the grim ramparts," the style of *pietra dura* decoration is typical of the Jehangir era. Imagine it as the private apartments of two great and most beautiful queens, Nur Jahan and Mumtaz Mahal, complete with the most gorgeous Persian carpets, magnificent awnings, beautiful slave girls, a rippling stream playing down the marble fountain basin and with emperors as doting husbands. The Jasmine Tower still is the most splendid portion of the Agra fort. Here Shahjahan was to pass his last days in confinement looking at the Taj. Aurangzeb, his son, ensured that Shahjahan did not move out, had no external contact and for company and for someone to nurse his deteriorating health had only his daughter Jehanara and his memories of the dead queen.

Right: Interior of the Musamman Burj with a marble basin, Red Fort, Agra. Opposite page, Top: A pavilion with copper canopy, part of the royal enclosure near Khas Mahal, Red Fort, Agra.

1. Amar Singh Gate
2. Delhi Gate
3. Hathi Pol
4. Jehangiri Mahal
5. Diwan-i-Aam
6. Machli Bhawan
7. Diwan-i-Khas
8. Musamman Burj
9. Khas Mahal and Anguri Bagh
10. Sheesh Mahal
11. Moti Mosque
12. Palace
13. Terrace
14. Barbican Barbican
15. River Yamuna
16. Water Gate

The Red Fort from the river front.

PLAN OF AGRA FORT

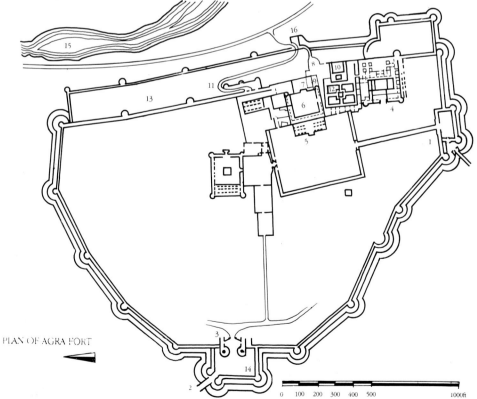

0   100 200 300 400 500   1000ft

The Diwan-i-Khas stands on a terrace over Musamman Burj. It is a small but grand hall, with double marble columns decorated with excellent floral motifs at the base, but much damaged by Jat vandals. On the terrace are two stone thrones. The black throne was made for Salim, who could sit and enjoy elephant fights on the riverfront of the fort walls.

Machchi Bhawan or Fish House facing the Diwan-i-Khas is actually a huge sunken courtyard with pavilions on all sides for the harem. The northern entrance to this enclosure is decorated with gateways plundered from Chittore, following Akbar's victory over the most impregnable of Rajput forts. At the north-west corner stands a small mosque for the private use of the royal ladies and later for Shahjahan when he was a prisoner at Musamman Burj. Meena Bazar where queens, princesses and ladies of the harem could enjoy a free bargain with the Emperor and princesses lies on the northern corners through Chittore gates. There Jehangir met Nur Mahal who was later titled Nur Jahan, and Shahjahan met Arjamand Bano, the future lady of the Taj.

Concealed steps lead to the Diwan-i-Aam, the magnificent hall of public audience with tall, elegant sandstone columns plastered over and coated with the finest lime and gold-lined. Many a proud *raja* stood here, head bent in obeisance to the Mughal Emperor. Ambassadors and emissaries presented their credentials here and rows of nobles and grandees stood silent in the presence of the king. Tavernier, the visitor to the Mughal Court, gives a graphic account of the proceedings at the Diwan-i-Aam. The Emperor acted as "the Shadow of God," and courtiers stood quietly in front of the royal throne which was triple arched and richly decorated.

Further north is the Moti Masjid (1648-55), a magnificent mosque in white marble built by Shahjahan. The red sandstone exterior contrasts with the dazzling white interior. Moti Masjid is famous for its admirable proportions and a harmonious blend of structural features including three marble domes surrounded by a string of small cupolas.

The ancient well in front of the Diwan-i-Aam and Salimgarh, a small double storey pavilion in red sandstone, now closed to the public, are the only reminders of the pre-Mughal Lodi occupation of the fort. If the fort contains only a few palaces of Akbar, it is because Jehangir and Shahjahan demolished many old structures on the eastern riverfront to be replaced by newer palaces and pavilions in marble.

Fatehpur Sikri Soon after his accession to the throne in Delhi, Akbar shifted his capital to Agra. He consolidated the young empire established by Babur and Humayun, and cemented his relations with the Rajputs by marrying into their families. But he was without an heir. However, the blessings of Sheikh Salim Chisti of Sikri led to the birth of his first son, Salim, named after the saint. In gratitude to the saint, Akbar also decided to build a new city on the ridge where the saint lived. The ridge overlooked the plain where Akbar's grandfather Babur had given battle to Rana Sanga and his Rajput allies to free the infant Mughal kingdom from a continuous threat to its security. Akbar's choice of the site was a delayed expression of thanks to his grandfather. The silent and barren hills of Sikri resounded with the hammer and chisel of thousands of artisans drawn from distant lands and a whole new population moved towards the hilltop, where, amid spacious courtyards palaces were rising, giving shape to an imperial vision. This was the city of Sikri, called Fatehpur after Akbar's conquests in Gujarat and the Deccan.

The palaces, pavilions and mosques reflect the power of the Mughal empire. Blending the best of both the Mughal and Rajput architectural traditions, the Sikri buildings are a true synthesis of two vastly different but perfect traditions. It was at Sikri that Akbar held discourses with mullahs, sadhus and priests. Islamic, Hindu and Jesuit missionaries sat with him in frequent and prolonged discussions, which led Akbar to formulate the *Din-i-Ilahi*, a new composite religion. Through the corridors of Sikri blew winds of understanding and compassion though some conservative heads shook in disapproval. But Akbar certainly knew how to keep his people pleased and together. He was a diplomat *par excellence* and determined not to lose a real kingdom for an unreal one.

As one enters from the Agra Gate, one of the nine stately gateways guarding entry to the city, the first building is the Diwan-i-Aam, where Akbar sat in public audience, listened to petitions, dispensed justice and watched entertainment programmes. It is an extensive courtyard enclosed by arcaded passages on three sides. The royal balcony, set within two

Opposite page: Musamman Burj, Red Fort, Agra.

FATEHPUR SIKRI COMPLEX

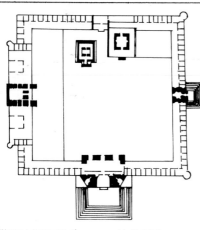

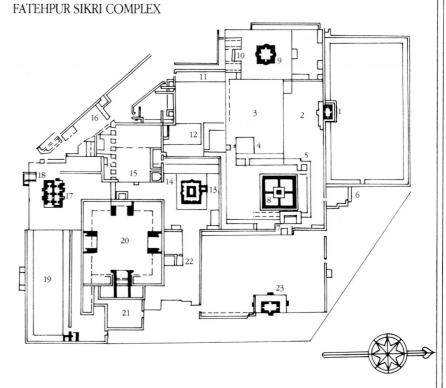

1. Diwan-i-Am (court of public audience)
2. Turkish Sultana's garden
3. Pachisi Court (court of games)
4. Girl's school
5. Turkish Sultana's house
6. Turkish Sultana's bath
7. Khwabgah (Emperor's sleeping quarters)
8. Char chaman
9. Diwan-i-Khas (court of private audience)
10. Ankh michauli (Emperor's study)
11. Hospital
12. Panch Mahal
13. Miriam's house
14. Miriam's bath
15. Miriam's garden
16. Nagina Masjid
17. Birbal's house
18. Hospital
19. Stables
20. Jodha Bai's palace
21. Bath
22. Guardhouse
23. Daftar Khana (administration and archives)

jali-work screens, is imposing. Akbar's presence was enough to inspire awe and confidence in the people.

In front of the royal seat a stone hook is embedded in the ground. According to legend, Akbar's pet elephant Hiran was tied here to crush to death under its feet the heads of the guilty. If the beast refused to obey three times, the victim was freed. It was believed that the elephant's will expressed the will of God. Huge crowds would come to the Darbar to have a look at Akbar, who had built an entire city on the deserted hills, a city larger than contemporary London. The Diwan-i-Khas, where Akbar held legal, political and religious discussions, is a small structure in the courtyard behind the Diwan-i-Aam. Externally a double storey structure, this is actually a single storey hall with a high, flat ceiling. It contains the most ornamental piece of Mughal architecture, a central column which bursts forth into a set of thirty-six closely set voluted and pendulous brackets topped with a circular platform from which radiate four passages. Tradition has it that Akbar's *Din-i-Ilahi* was formulated on the royal seat above this column.

The royal treasury stands next to the Diwan-i-Khas. The arrangement of three inter-connected rooms with secret lockers, built within recesses in the walls, contained the gold and silver and state regalia. A small kiosk outside draws many anxious looks for its ornate *torana* decoration, typical of Jain architecture. It is also believed to be the room of the court astrologer. Some even believe Akbar played hide-and-seek here with his numerous wives, though this is a far-fetched guess. However, in the courtyard facing this kiosk Akbar played *pachisi* with his slave girls.

On the western line of this courtyard stands Panch Mahal, a five-storeyed pavilion which looks like the skeleton of some magnificent edifice. It is a Persian wind tower where harem ladies could come to enjoy the morning and evening breeze. The differently shaped pillars on each floor are elegant and superbly sculptured. The *jali* screens which once provided the purdah (cover) for the ladies were removed during renovations at the beginning of this century. The top floor offers magnificent views of the Sikri landscape and the meandering fortifications.

At the southern corner of this royal courtyard lies Anup Talao, the tank where, on the central platform, the legendary Tansen, Akbar's court musician, played marvellous ragas. Originally the tank was twelve feet deep but filled up to its present level in the last century. The Emperor's living quarters are built on the opposite side. The stone platform raised on stone columns was the royal bed and the small window used for *jharokha darshan*. There were many who would not eat or drink water till they saw the king's face. With few decorations, this palace also contained the royal library and rare manuscripts and paintings.

But the most attractive structure here is the Turkish Sultana palace, built for Akbar's queen of Turkish descent. A small room surrounded by a covered verandah, the red sandstone surface of the walls, eaves and dados, in fact, every available inch of space, is elegantly sculptured into exquisite geometric and floral patterns. This most excellent ornamentation shows a strong Chinese influence–chiselling the flat wall surface into panels of finesse.

Gold Coins found at Fatehpur Sikri

Jodha Bai's palace is a high walled, sombre looking edifice, guarded by an impressive gateway. The harem quarters built around the great courtyard provided the utmost privacy to the queens and princesses. The columns are decorated with bell and chain motifs, heavy ornamental brackets and niches on walls to house images of Hindu deities worshipped by the inmates of the harem. The *tulsi* plant was kept in the small stone tank-like structure in the centre of the courtyard. Today, Jodha Bai's palace stands deserted and forlorn but once it contained all the splendour of a royal harem.

Another small structure – Miriam Makani's palace, has some surviving traces of mural decorations and was meant for Hamida Banu, Akbar's mother. Behind this palace lie gardens for the harem ladies.

Behind Jodha Bai's palace stands a small double-storeyed building with exquisitely carved walls and elegant brackets. It is believed to have belonged to Birbal, one of the nine gems of Akbar's court, but it is a little too close to the harem quarters to have been the house of the minister. The royal stables are built in front of this house.

The northern corner of Sikri city contains a small mosque for ladies and a *langar khana* (alms house). The narrow road leads to Hathi Pol, a gateway guarded by two statues of col-

Opposite page, Top: Buland Darwaza, Fatehpur Sikri, Agra.

ossal elephants standing on high pedestals with intertwined trunks. The statues are much damaged but the gateway is still grand, fit for the royal procession to enter the city. The huge sprawling lake has now dried up. The *baoli* outside the Hathi Pol formed part of the Sikri waterworks and the octagonal structure is still in a good state of preservation. Traces of pipelines and aquaducts can still be seen at a few places. The Hiran Minar, built on a high platform, is believed to commemorate Akbar's favourite elephant. It is notable for the one thousand stone tusks decorating the tower.

Turning back into the city, take the right turn. Here lie the ruins of many utilitarian structures, caravanserais, stables, schools etc. The only building of some beauty is the grand mansion of Abul Fazl and his brother Faizi, standing enclosed within a compound under the shadow of the Sikri mosque.

The mosque at Sikri is built on the highest point of the ridge. The courtyard could accommodate ten thousand worshippers. The eastern gate was meant for use by royalty. The three domes of the mosque are modest in size but elegant. However, this mosque is not known for its external grandeur so much as for the splendid ornamentation of its sanctum. Modelled after Bibi Khanam's mosque at Samarkand, this is the grandest mosque amongst Akbar's buildings. For to look at the walls, arches, ceilings, *mihrab*, and anywhere that the eye roves, you only see an unexcelled painted magnificence. In the early mornings, when the rays of the sun cast light on the stone floor, the whole interior brightens up with a grandeur of its own.

The exquisite little tomb of Sheikh Salim Chisti is the only structure in white marble in this courtyard and is surrounded by red sandstone colonnades. The *jali* screens at the tomb of the saint, made of single slabs of marble, are exquisite pieces of the highest craftsmanship. The struts or bracket pillars in the porch have also been carved out of single marble blocks. The serpentine volutes show a fascinating perfection in marble craft. But the best part of the tomb is the ebony frame over the grave covered with mother-of-pearl. In the dimly lit interior, the cenotaph chamber glows with a rare splendour. The original crypt lies in the basement chamber where visitors are not allowed. Those longing for a child come here, pray, and tie a red cotton thread on the *jali*. They come again when the wish is granted.

The saint died in 1571 and Akbar built this tomb ten years later. In a few years time the Emperor left Sikri for good. The city was abandoned, but not the tomb of the saint. It still remains the most living part of the city for there rests the spirit of a saint who brought light to humanity and now "he is portion of the loveliness which once he made more lovely."

In 1575 Akbar added the Buland Darwaza, the last and the most spectacular gateway on the southern wall of the mosque. The Buland Darwaza commemorates Akbar's triumphant return after the conquest of Gujarat. It is a towering portal with a height of 134 feet over the top step and 176 feet over ground level. This red sandstone gateway is Persian in concept with the arched facade dominating the landscape for miles. The arabesque decoration and lotus motifs create a rare synthesis of divergent architectural styles. The giant-size doorway is covered with horseshoes and bits of metals – offerings of those who come to wish for the recovery of their ailing animals. The saint within has to look after this as well.

An inscription in Naskh carries a message: "The world is but a bridge: pass over but build no houses on it." The king, whose pride inspired him to build this loftiest gateway, had still some humility left in him.

To the west of Buland Darwaza are some old structures, derelict and much damaged. The water reservoir is still used as a public bath and for a small reward young boys will dive into the water from a staggering height. The small place where Jodha Bai gave birth so Salim is now much altered and houses a workshop. The stone cutter's mosque, the first structure built after construction at Sikri started, is a derelict site. The stone *baradari* of Raja Todar Mal stands beyond the city limits. It is now in sheer ruins.

This is not all. Look anywhere and you will notice tottering ruins in a frightening wilderness.

Fatehpur Sikri was abandoned by Akbar within fifteen years of its construction in 1585. Some suggest because the climate was unsuitable, some think because the saint had died Akbar felt lonely without his spiritual guide. Or perhaps the growing empire required a more central place as the capital. Jehangir and Shahjahan paid a few visits to Sikri, but for all practical purposes the days of glory for Fatehpur Sikri were over after 1585. It has remained

Mughal Emperor Jehangir

Opposite page: Top: The great inner courtyard, Fatehpur Sikri, Agra. Bottom: Sculptured dado panel at the Turkish Sultana Palace, Fatehpur Sikri, Agra. Following page: View of the Panch Mahal from the astrologer's seat, Fatehpur Sikri, Agra.

the world's best preserved ghost city for centuries now.

Sikandra The tomb of Akbar, the greatest Mughal Emperor, stands on the north-western edge of Agra, five kms beyond Delhi Gate on the Agra-Delhi Road. Excepting the Taj Sikandra may well be Agra's most spectacular monument. Long before the city is reached, the four minarets of the entrance gate of the tomb rise over the tree tops and the first full view of the gateway leaves you stunned at its grandeur.

It is believed that Akbar started construction work on the tomb in his lifetime, a tradition established by his predecessors. When he died the work was still in progress and his son Jehangir thought of his father's tomb rather late. An inscription on the southern gateway states: "In the seventh year of the august succession of Jehangir, corresponding to A.H. 1021, seven years of work attained completion." This was the year 1613.

A contemporary traveller, William Finch, recorded in 1611 that the construction had actually begun ten years prior to his visit and that the arch of the gateway was complete then: "The tomb was not finished at my departure, but lay in a manner of a coffin. Covered with a white sheet, interwrought with gold and flowers," and added that, "The tomb was to be inarched over the most curious white and speckled marble, to be all with pure sheet gold richly inwrought." The intention of a central dome over the topmost marble terrace was left unaccomplished. Till today the whole structure stands asking for it.

The impact of Akbar's tastes shows in the understated looks of the three lower storeys in red sandstone as at Agra and Sikri. His dilettante son Jehangir preferred delicate white marble for the top storey, a rather ill-matched fancy dressing for the sturdy body. The mausoleum proper is built on the northern side of the garden. The structure is pyramidal. Some believe it was inspired by Buddhist Vihar architecture and some even trace a Cambodian influence. Not improbable theoretically, but somewhat far-fetched in reality.

Opposite page: The incredible splendour of craftsmanship on lattice screens at Salim Chisti's Dargah at Fatehpur Sikri, Agra. Left: Nav Rattan Pillar with four radiating passages at the Diwan-i-Khas, Fatehpur Sikri, Agra.

It is through the central archway on the ground floor that you enter the cenotaph chamber and pass through the vestibule decorated with the most magnificent ornamentation in stucco. The gold and blue colours are still gorgeous. The sepulchre is in simple and unpretentious white marble in a gesture of humility and submission to the will of Allah. The Jats plundered the tomb and took away gold and jewels, the Emperor's armour, clothes and books originally placed beside the sarcophagus. This happened when the Mughal empire was in decline. The gun metal lamp hanging from the ceiling was presented by Lord Curzon in 1905, the only decoration in this chamber.

The topmost terrace is entirely in white marble with ingenuously crafted trellis screens that are dignified and exquisite. The marble pedestal held the lamp near the cenotaph which was cast out of a single block of marble. Covered with floral ornamentation, it bears the words "Allaho Akbar", meaning "Great is Allah's Glory."

Sikandra was built during the period of transition from Akbar's stone work to the highly sensuous and luxuriant marble edifices of Jehangir and Shahjahan. Jehangir disapproved of the style of work at Sikandra and much of it was pulled down on his orders.

On the ground floor the tall pylon of the entrance dominates clusters and galleries meant for Akbar's household. Out of the 44 chambers only four are occupied.

Between the tomb and entrance gate stretches the 123-acre sprawling garden laid in the typical Persian plan with the whole sweep of the flagged causeways, each expanded at a suitable interval into a square terrace containing a fountain and a sunk basin. The high wall surrounding the garden has four gateways. The southern gateway with minarets is the most ornamented and fully completed. The northern gateway is in complete ruins. The eastern and western gateways are in a good state of preservation with sumptuous floral murals.

The southern gateway is an architectural achievement of exceptional merit, elegance and splendour. The four minarets are superb, gorgeous *pietra dura* work on the spandrels of the arches and floral mosaics cover the entire surface of the gateway. Later, at Itmad-ud-daula and the Taj, this ornamentation reached its perfect culmination. As Bamber Gascoigne observes, this gateway is "a complete success architecturally". The minarets, damaged by

Right: The Jama Masjid at Fatehpur Sikri, Agra. Opposite page: Top: Dargah of Sheikh Salim Chisti at Fatehpur Sikri, Agra. Bottom, Left: The brackets in the porch of Salim Chisti's Dargah, Fatehpur Sikri, Agra. Right: Hiran Minar, Fatehpur Sikri, Agra.

Akbar's Tomb at Sikandra, Agra.

lightning, were restored by the British engineers in the last century.

In an ironical twist of destiny, the insurgent Jats looted Sikandra in 1688 and considerably damaged the grave, without realizing that they were desecrating the memory of the most liberal Mughal who hated bigotry as much as they did. Still what survives today at Sikandra is the most spectacular Mughal tomb.

Itmad-ud-daula In 1626, Nur Jahan built an elegant tomb for her father on the other side of the Yamuna, near the fruit garden laid by Babur. This small structure stands within a high-walled enclosure 540 feet high, pierced by four grand gateways, one on each side. The western gateway is on the river front. This mausoleum became a landmark in the history of Mughal architecture as marking the transition from the red sandstone masculine architecture of Akbar to the exquisitely ornamented white marble work of Jehangir and Shahjahan. The mausoleum is square, 70 feet in diameter on a raised platform. The cenotaph chamber is a rectangular hall surrounded by four octagonal corner rooms and interconnecting vestibules. The ceiling and the walls above the dado level are lavishly decorated with murals of geometric designs and floral motifs. The rectangular corner towers are topped by cupolas. Enclosed within screens of lattice work, a small pavilion on the flat-roofed second storey rests over this jewel-box of a structure.

Structurally important are the cornices, brackets and broad eaves which provide shade to a fascinating mix of light and shade on the dazzling white marble inlaid with textured and coloured precious stones. The tombstones are built in marble of a green-yellow hue, rather gorgeous for a tomb. The floor is also magnificent, a Persian carpet of inlaid stone. It is not the *pietra dura* use of coloured stone pieces in the sculpted hollows of marble as at Sikandra, but the use of precious stones like lapis, onyx, jasper, topaz and cornelian in the exquisite floral forms done with an for detail which only a masterful eye for delicacy could obtain.

The garden is laid out in the Mughal Char Bagh style and is further ordered into four smaller squares. The four red sandstone gateways have been decorated with beautiful mosaics in white and coloured marble in contrast with the main edifice in marble which is reflected in the water canal, part of the garden.

Nur Jahan, Jehangir's queen, was an exceptional beauty as well as an astute administrator. Her father, a courtier who had fled the Persian court, benefitted much from his daughter whom he had left behind in poverty and later regained. He became the prime minister to Jehangir and was titled Itmad-ud-daula (Pillar of the State). She decided to build a mausoleum befitting her father's status in pure silver, but which, for fear of thieves, was ultimately made in white marble.

The Itmad-ud-daula tomb is not important for its proportions. It is known for the surface ornamentation, the naturalistic floral designs, wine bottles, fruits and cypresses in the Persian style. The beautiful stones studded into the marble's surface were chosen for the feel of their texture so that when felt with eyes closed, the mosaics feel like "an architecture of braille."

The cenotaph chamber lies in semi-darkness and the splendour of the painted ceiling remains half-hidden from the eye. In the neighbourhood of Itmad-ud-daula stands Chinia Roza, a tomb in tiles. Built in 1635, it belongs to Allama Afzal Khan Mullah Shukrullah of Shiraz, poet, counsellor and later prime minister in Shahjahan's court. The octagonal structure is now in complete ruins. Surface repairs done to prevent a sudden collapse have left out certain portions of ornamentation in turquoise, blue, green, yellow and mauve tiles in the authentic Persian style. No other tomb or structure in Agra or Delhi carries such splendid decorations, which in its heyday must have been unparalleled in grandeur. The surviving portions testify to their original splendour. In this single-chamber high-domed hall where the tomb lies shorn of the slightest cover of marble or red sandstone the high double-dome, beyond the reach of vandals, still looks grand and impressive.

Jama Masjid One of the best mosques in the city is the Jama Masjid, built by Jehanara Begum in 1648. This mosque is conspicuous for the absence of minarets, a familiar component of Mughal mosques. The squat domes in red sandstone are ornamented with marble lines in "a zig-zag" pattern. The long line of cupolas in the northern and southern walls contribute a distinctive charm of its own. It is Agra's most frequented mosque, surrounded by a

busy market.

Taj Mahal The Taj, the most beautiful, the most romantic, the most enigmatic and the most photographed building in the world remains Shahjahan's greatest gift to the cultural heritage of the world. It is the most magnificent building ever built by man. Come any time of the day, any day of the year, in the blistering summer months, or the freezing winter, or during the rainy monsoons, the Taj is always full of visitors, lovers, newlyweds, the old and the young, rich and poor. They all come here to see for themselves the achievement of an Emperor inspired by love for his dead queen. They have all heard that the Taj is beautiful beyond words: and so it is today as it has been since 1652, when the white pearl dome raised its head against the azure sky, "proud passion of an Emperor's love," as Edwin Arnold calls it. No one is disappointed with the Taj. The first view of the mausoleum framed within the dark arched entrance is enchanting.

But facts first. Shahjahan, when only a prince, was captivated by the charms of Nur Jahan's niece Arjamand Bano, and married her. She was titled Mumtaz Mahal, "Exalted one of the Palace". She died in 1631, while giving birth to his fourteenth child. But he had promised her two things – no more children and the most beautiful memorial ever built by a man for his woman. Within six months of her death, he brought her body from Burhanpur in the Deccan, where she had breathed her last, to Agra, gave her another temporary burial near the river and started work on a building which, as time and history have proved, was to be the world's most magnificent memorial.

Shahjahan harnessed all the resources at his command to procure the most expensive and the most beautiful material for the tomb. White marble from Makrana near Jodhpur, cornelian from Baghdad, turquoise from Tibet and Persia, malachite from Russia, diamonds and onyx from Central Asia. Nearly 20,000 men and women worked for twelve years, supervised by the greatest masters of their craft, Ustad Ahmad Lahori, chief architect, Mulla Mushid from Persia, Muhammad Afandi from Turkey. The Emperor had visited the best architectural sites of India and seems to have approved of the basic structures of the tomb of Humayun, his great grandfather, and Abdul Rahim Khan-i-Khan, both in Delhi. The design was purely indigenous and Shahjahan personally supervised work, looking after the minutest details. The result of this unique enterprise of love and fidelity was that vision of loveliness known as the Taj Mahal.

The entrance gateway, the most magnificent portal to any building, stands midway in the general plan of structures at the Taj. Approached through a line of arcaded galleries which served as markets and *serais* with three smaller gateways guarding entry to the precincts, this massive gateway is itself an architectural achievement of no small merit. The red sandstone structure has a grand arched facade framed within a rectangular frame of calligraphic decoration verses from the 89th chapter of the Quran, and the twenty-six cupolas in white marble on top lend it an air of royal dignity. The floral arabesques on the spandrel of the arch are only a token of the beauty of similar decoration at the mausoleum proper contained within. An inscription reads: "So enter as one of his servants; and enter into His garden." This is the gateway to the garden of Paradise on earth, the end of the profane and the beginning of the sacred area. The huge doors of solid silver and the 110 nails topped by Shahjahan's silver coins which adorned this gateway were plundered by the Jats when the Mughal empire fell into decline in the eighteenth century. The present brass door was made in the following century.

The first view of the Taj from this arched entrance is the most famous one. The Taj is still some 900 feet away, floating, as it were, above the ground, traversed by countless men and women. It is an ingenious manipulation of perspective from this vantage point. The massive marble dome of the Taj seems so close, drawing the visitor irresistibly towards it. Immediately below this entrance gateway lies the water canal with its splendid fountains, stretching upto the mausoleum proper. The garden has been laid in the familiar Char Bagh style. This axial channel leads to Hauz-i-Kausar the elevated pool at the centre of the four quarters of the garden. The four big squares are further sub-divided into four squares making it sixteen squares. Each plot was orginally planted with four hundred flower plants. The water courses and central raised lotus pool mirror to perfection the grandeur of the tomb. The cypresses along the canal symbolize death and the trees in blossom, life.

The high walls surrounding the garden are in red sandstone and provide a fitting contrast

Opposite page, Top: Tomb of Itmad-ud-daula, built by Nur Jahan, Agra. Bottom: Jama Masjid built by Jehanara Begum, Agra.

to the sprawling, rich greenery. Here was that oasis of luxury of greenery and water, fruit trees and fountains which for these Timurid warriors from the deserts of Central Asia was the very promised Paradise.

Tantalizingly, the dome beckons the visitor from any corner of the garden. As you approach the mausoleum, parts of this white ghost seem to reveal the full magnitude of their proportions, displaying the classical purity of architecture uncluttered by any fanciful designing.

The mausoleum stands on a marble platform 22 feet in height and 313 feet square. The red sandstone platform is itself nearly six or seven feet high to raise the structure above eye level. An elegant flight of steps leads to the marble platforms where you are on a different plane altogether, uplifted as if were. The building proper is a square with its corners cut off to form an octagon, further fashioned to form smaller octagon with the central octagon containing the cenotaphs. This is the typical Persian plan, earlier adopted at Humayun's and Khan-i-Khana's tombs in Delhi.

Notice the rectangle framing the keel arch—a shape repeated at various places in various forms: gateways, Iwan, niches, trellised doors, windows, dome, ornamental band, cusped arches of cupolas, turrets surrounding corner towers and the podium on which the mausoleum stands. The arch remains central to the design of the Taj as it is in Islamic architecture in general, and imbuing it with a renewed spiritual force are the bands of Quranic inscriptions, superbly calligraphed in Naskh by Abdul Haq Shirazi. The whole Quran has been inscribed on these four recessed arches at the Taj. The calligraphed lettering appears of the same size, from the bottom to the top but, in fact, the letters grow bigger with the increasing height. It is an ingenious display of the art of calligraphy, man's nearest approach to Allah.

The walls of the mausoleum look plain dazzling white but if you look patiently, a whole new world of superb, low-key ornamentation unfolds itself before you. The dado panels, framed with elegant lilies and tulips, contain the white marble iris – the flower of death. These panels adorn the lower sections of walls all around the mausoleum.

Enter the mausoleum through the southern arch. The octagonal chamber below the dome contains the cenotaphs of Mumtaz Mahal in the centre and Shahjahan to her left. The dappled shadows cast a mysterious halo here and as your eyes adjust themselves to the semi-darkness around the exquisite and the most perfect *pietra dura* ornamentation on these tombstones glimmers in all its incredible grandeur. The beauty of the inlay work is legendary. Thirty-five types of precious stones have been used and a single flower can contain upto 60 pieces of cornelian. Under torchlight the splendour of the coloured stones is even more marvellous. The gravestone of Mumtaz is marked by a slate and Shahjahan's by a male penbox.

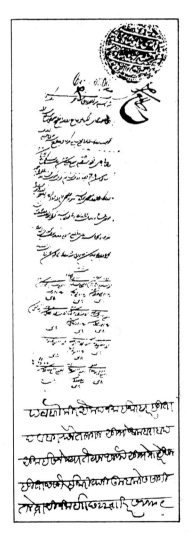

These cenotaphs were originally enclosed within a gold railing encrusted with precious stones and a pearl canopy hung over the grave of Mumtaz. For fear of vandalism, Aurangzeb had these removed and replaced with the present marble lattice screens. These screens are perhaps the finest and most perfect specimens of artistry, the most magnificent part of the mausoleum, worth their weight in gold and much more, "a triumph of Oriental decorative art."

The original lamp over these cenotaphs was removed by the Jats and Lord Curzon had a new Cairene lamp made for this chamber, which is lighted softly by the light filtering through the marble screens in the arches of the passage enclosing the cenotaphs, the subsidiary chamber and the radiating passages.

Below these cenotaphs, in a similar octagonal hall lie the real gravestones of the royal couple, serene and peaceful in their final rest. The gravestones carry *pietra dura* work of unexcelled quality, the pride of Mughal architecture. The magnificent Persian carpets and royal paraphernalia were all taken away by the Jats, but the gravestones and the marble screens escaped their greedy hands.

The interior of the cenotaph chamber lies under a double dome over a double-storeyed interior The Taj interior looks quite intimate.

And, so again to the platform, where perforce the dome dominates the view. The height from the base of the drum on which the marble pearl-shaped dome is built, to the top of the finial is 145 feet (44 metres). The magnitude of this superstructure is reduced by the four

Opposite page: Taj Mahal, the most enchanting first full view of the great mausoleum, Agra. Above: Portrait of Shahjahan, and reproduction of an interesting manuscript of the Chihl-Majlis, which contains the signature of Shahjahan under the Royal Seal.

Above: Portrait of Queen Mumtaz Mahal, in whose memory Taj Mahal was built. Right: Taj Mahal.

smaller cupolas and the four slim, small minarets which seem to guard this marvel. From early morning to late evening hours the dome reflects the changing mood of light and the white Makrana gleams in various hues. The convex swell of the dome and the concave recessed arches manipulate light and shadow to great dramatic effect. The dome looks like a pearl. The throne of God in Paradise is surmounted by a huge pearl supported by four corner pillars. The dome symbolizes the vault of heaven and the octagon supporting it represents transition from the material world. The pearl also symbolizes the female charm and the dome of the Taj is "the apotheosis of Indian Womanhood, a radiant architectural embodiment of all that is feminine..." The minarets standing at the four corners of the marble platform provide a fitting frame to the noble edifice. These tapering minarets, 137 feet in height, are topped by a shallow umbrella dome, and seem to carry forward the style of the great dome over the mausoleum.

The Taj enclosure is bound by two grand buildings in red sandstone: the mosque on its west and a guesthouse on its eastern sides. Removed from the Taj setting these two structures would still be magnificent, assured of their place in the best examples of Mughal architecture.

The Taj is at its best in the early hours of the day when it appears like a beauty emerging out of her slumber, the soft moulding of its contours silhouetted against the soft crimson of the sky; then with the first rays of the sun the minarets and the dome come alive with an enthralling radiance. The marble glows and shines, clothed in the pearly light of the early sun. As the sun rises high in the sky, the white marble acquires a fierce dazzle, still enchanting, still attractive. In the afternoon, the mellow orange tinge does wonders to the mausoleum, which renews its charm. At sunset, the beauty of the Taj is irresistible and as darkness spreads its cover all over the landscape, you can feel it – the Taj is still there. The Taj is the very quintessence of love.

Take a boat ride from the fort and approach the Taj as Shahjahan used to. On a closer look the mausoleum appears like a mirage reflected in the quiet waters of the Yamuna which takes a sharp bend around the Taj. A village has sprung up where Shahjahan once planned a black marble replica of the Taj for himself. Sadly, he died too soon, heartbroken at Aurangzeb's behaviour, who killed his three other sons and kept him a prisoner in Musamman Burj with only Jehanara for company. The ruins of the basement structures now have been exposed to the common gaze. Wells on which the foundations of a giant structure were to be built, stand out of the sand at places where the river has changed its course. The solitary pavilion, a long wall, some plinth level solid structures are all there to be seen, the only evidence of the great subterranean structures required to build a massive mausoleum. Shahjahan was buried beside Mumtaz Mahal in the Taj itself, the only asymmetrical point in a building which in every aspect of its construction is as perfect a model of symmetry as of incredible finesse of craftsmanship and design. As the river waters lap the basement walls of the Taj, you know it is a reality after all, not the creation of sheer romantic fancy. In fact, the Taj is a metaphor of love in white marble.

Opposite page: The tomb of Mumtaz Mahal, lady of the Taj.

Below: Close-up view of the splendid calligraphic and floral ornamentation of the Taj Mahal. Right: Inlay work at the Taj Mahal. Far right: The Taj Mahal reflected in the river.

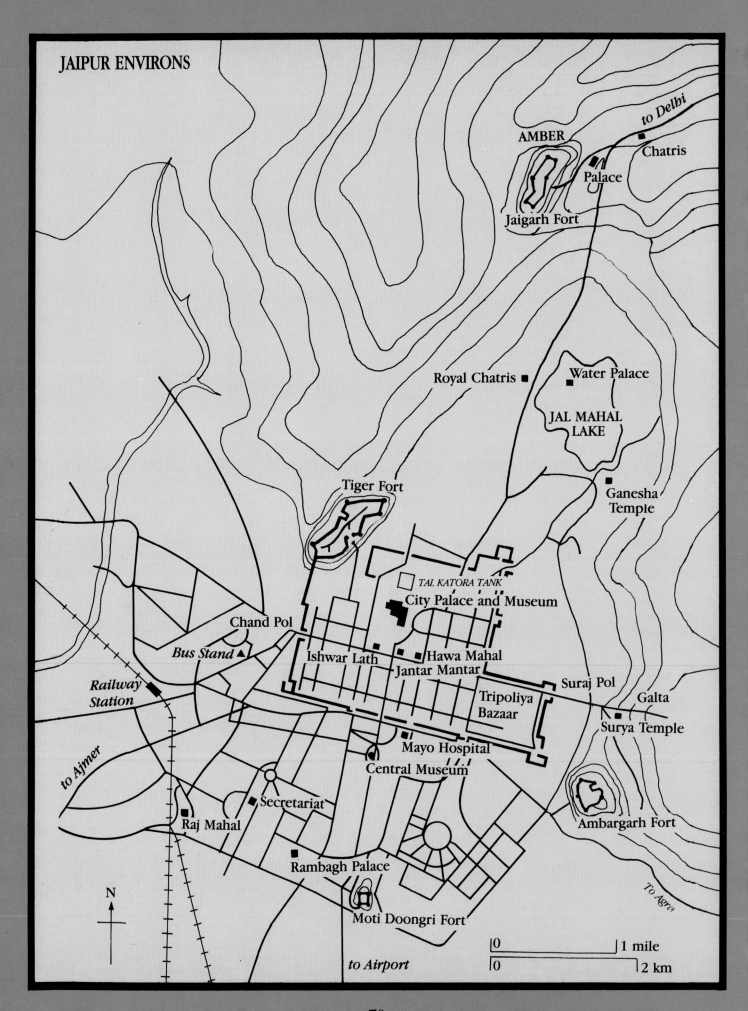

JAIPUR ENVIRONS

to Delhi

AMBER

Chatris

Palace

Jaigarh Fort

Royal Chatris

Water Palace

JAL MAHAL LAKE

Ganesha Temple

Tiger Fort

TAL KATORA TANK

City Palace and Museum

Chand Pol

Bus Stand

Ishwar Lath

Hawa Mahal

Jantar Mantar

Suraj Pol

Galta

Railway Station

Tripoliya Bazaar

Surya Temple

to Ajmer

Mayo Hospital

Central Museum

Secretariat

Ambargarh Fort

Raj Mahal

To Agra

Rambagh Palace

N

Moti Doongri Fort

to Airport

|0   1 mile

|0   2 km

70

Jaipur

City of Forts & Palaces

Jaipur is a charming city; rugged and romantic. Built in 1727 Jaipur lies at the foot of the Kalikoh hill, watched over by Nahargarh Fort. Though it is now getting industrialized it has retained a fairy tale charm. Magnificent forts crowning the hills provide a grand background to the Pink City. Womenfolk proudly move around decked in dazzling silver jewellery and bright coloured swirling skirts, blouses and *odhnis*. Men wear white dhoti folded over the knees and a tight shirt topped by a gorgeous turban. Jaipur is a queer blend of the exotic and the modern with its exquisite medieval architecture in a modern setting.

Amber As a city Jaipur was preceded by the quintessentially medieval Amber, the capital of the Kachhwaha Rajputs, descendants of Kusha, son of Rama, the king of Ayodhya. In 295 A.D. these Rajputs moved from Rohtas to Narwar near Gwalior. Success and prosperity followed their valourous campaigns. But in 967 A.D. Dhola Rae, infant heir to the throne, was banished from Narwar by his uncle who usurped power. Dhola and his queen mother ran west to save their lives.

The former queen found a menial job with a Mina chief, who later adopted her as his sister. When Dhola grew up, he killed his benefactor and assumed independent power which he augmented by marital alliances with a Bargujar family (descendants of Lav, another son of Rama) and an Ajmer princess. But fate did not permit him a long tenure. He was killed by the Minas.

Marooni, Dhola's widow, gave birth to Kankhal, who grew up to win the Dhundhar territory and his son later annexed Amber from the Susawat Minas. So the Kachhwahas came to settle at Amber, though their quarrels with the Minas remained a recurring feature of their lives. Pajun, Udaikarna and Prithviraj, illustrious Kachhwaha rulers, earned great renown for the dynasty which was to see much greater fame when the Mughals appeared as founders of a great empire.

After Bahar Mal or Behari Mal (1548-74) became the ruler, the history of Amber appears in a clear light. On his way to Ajmer in January 1562, Akbar invited the whole family of Bahar Mal to attend the royal camp. This association was cemented when Akbar married Bahar Mal's daughter, a matrimonial alliance which secured the Kachhwahas against regular skirmishes with the recalcitrant Minas. The Mughal Emperor could also expect peaceful association with other Rajput princes warring against him. Bahar Mal's daughter later gave birth to Salim, who became the heir to Akbar's throne. Bhagwan Das, who succeeded Bahar Mal, continued a reconciliatory policy towards the Mughals.

These were the early years of Amber palace atop the hill. Some rudimentary structures had been built, but it was Man Singh I who really fortified it and adorned it with magnificent palaces, reflected in the Maota Lake at the foot of the hill. The hills rising beyond the terraces on which Amber is built seem to provide a natural defence

Suraj Pol crowns the hill. This royal entrance is approached through a narrow winding road and leads to Jaleb Chowk, the grand courtyard where armies lined up before marching out. The double-storeyed pavilions, rows of rooms and high walls surrounding it lend grandeur to the whole setting. At the north-west corner of Jaleb Chowk stands the shrine of Sila Mata, or Kali Mandir, the most sacred shrine of the Kachhwaha rulers. It was built by Man Singh 1 in 1604 to install the image of the deity he had brought from Jessore in East Bengal. A family of Bengali priests also came to settle here. One of their descendants, Vidyadhar Bhattacharya, later became the chief architect of Jaipur. In 1939, Man Singh II added silver doors to the shrine.

Maharaja Jai Singh

The oldest portions of Amber palace stand at the southern end and are approached through long, narrow and dark passages built within walls suddenly opening into sun-filled courtyards.

The Zenana Palace, meant for the royal ladies, is a complex of rooms and apartments within the high-walled enclosure and triple-storeyed corner towers. A *baradari* in the central courtyard was the place for celebrations and entertainments. Man Singh's close association with Akbar helped him acquire knowledge of buildings at Agra and Sikri. The spartan simplicity of the rooms is relieved by vestiges of some frescoes depicting the frolics of Krishna. The Zenana Palace successors made no additions to this palace.

Jehangir's Rajput wife, Jodha Bai, bestowed the seat of Amber upon Jai Singh I, Man Singh I's nephew, and thereby hangs a tale. When commanded by the Mughal Emperor to *salaam* Jodha Bai, Jai Singh refused: "I will do this to any lady of Your Majesty's family, but not to Jodha Bai." The Queen took it in good humour saying, "It matters not, I give you the raj of Amber." This young prince was Jai Singh I with the title Mirza Raja. He decided to emulate his illustrious uncle Man Singh I in building grand new palaces in the style of the Mughals, ushering in an era of splendour at Amber.

The Diwan-i-Khas consists of two oblong chambers, adjoining rooms and an open verandah surrounding the main edifice. Also called Sheesh Mahal, the rooms are ornamented with millions of glass pieces in a mosaic stretching from floor to ceiling and creating a fabulous atmosphere as a lighted candle below the ceiling is reflected in myriad flickering forms above. Three stained glass windows add romantic colour to the chambers. The larger windows open towards the lake lying hundreds of feet below.

Sukh Niwas, built opposite Sheesh Mahal, was meant for ladies of the seraglio and courtesans as a cool haven, protecting them from the overpowering heat of the barren hills sloping down to the back walls of the palace. Ingenious water lifting devices filled the cistern placed atop the roof to fall in cascades over the chutes and run through the channels. A mixture of egg shells, pearls and powdered marble rendered the walls marble-smooth. Not as magnificent as the Sheesh Mahal, Sukh Niwas is nonetheless a palace of luxury. Both

Previous page: Amber Fort, Jaipur.
Right: Jaleb Chowk, the grand
courtyard at Amber Fort, Jaipur.
Opposite page: Glass mosaics at
Sheesh Mahal, Amber Fort, Jaipur.

Sheesh Mahal and Sukh Niwas open into a sunken garden with a star-shaped arrangement of passages leading to the central platform. It is a small but splendid garden.

On the roof of the Sheesh Mahal stands another small gem of a pavilion – Jas Mandir, luminescent with splendid glass mosaics, spangled mirrors and delicate colours. The windows, covered with the most exquisite triple-arched *jali* screens, open towards the lake, a vista of sheer romantic charm, particularly during the rains.

Jai Singh I had made it a habit to create small structures of scintillating charm. Close to Jas Mandir, on the same terrace, stands Sohag Mandir, a pavilion with lovely floral murals. The exceptionally fine trellis screens and small windows enabled royal ladies to watch the proceedings in the courtyard below.

A narrow ramp built within the thick walls descends into a grand courtyard where stand two structures of great magnificence. The Diwan-i-Aam, raised on a podium, is a rectangular hall with a double row of red sandstone pillars with carved elepnant heads as brackets. For fear of arousing the jealousy of Jehangir, Jai Singh I had it covered with plaster.

Ganesh Pol is the ceremonial portal to the maze of palaces and gardens contained within this high-walled enclosure. Its formidable exterior is covered with soft-hued murals of floral and geometric designs. The row of arches flanking the grand entrance adds to it a remarkable stateliness. Over the cusped, arched doorway has been painted the auspicious image of Ganesha. The smaller alcoves in the smaller arches carry rich ornamentation in subdued colours which shine in splendour in the early morning light. The Sukh Mandir trellis screens provide a fitting finish to the upper portion of Ganesh Pol, the most impressive gateway at Amber.

Both Man Singh I and Mirza Raja Jai Singh I built palaces of exceptional grandeur at Amber. Jai Singh I served Jehangir, Shahjahan and Aurangzeb betwen 1621 and 1667. In fact, he acted as the buffer between the intrepid Rajput rulers and the Mughals. He had ensured that Shivaji attended Aurangzeb's court but finding it impossible to keep his pledge of security to the Maratha chief, helped him escape the Mughal guards. He had become an influential diplomat, but a little too vain: He would hold two glasses in his hands, one of which he called Delhi, the other Satara, and dashing one to the ground, would exclaim, "There goes Satara; the fate of Delhi, is in my right hand and this with like felicity I can cast away." Aurangzeb resorted to the familiar Mughal device of removing an adversary and had Mirza Raja poisoned by his own son. Mirza Raja may be a forgotten politician, but he is the much remembered builder of the glorious Amber palaces.

Back at the Jaleb Chowk you must also make a small trip through Chand Pol to the back of the Amber palace. The fierce Kalikoh hills frown from their tops and the few deserted grand mansions of chiefs, counsellors and dignitaries stand clinging to the slopes. Their portals and courtyards speak of a fabulous past. A narrow path descends into the valley, where ruins of the ancient Amber can still be observed in derelict temples and decaying houses, cenotaphs. tanks, and sunken courtyards, crumbling stone walls lying beside the modern, small antennae-topped houses mushrooming all around.

The Jagat Shiromani Temple is the jewel of the ancient Amber city. Dedicated to Krishna, it has the image of Meera as the Lord's consort. The high ceiling of the vestibule contains glorious murals. The Shikhara (spire) of this temple is a soaring structure decorated with bands of sculptures. A Garuda temple in marble shares the platform. It is small but contains a wealth of superb sculptures. The *torana*, (triumphal arch), over the steps leading to this Krishna temple is flanked by statues of elephants.

The only mosque at Amber was built on Akbar's orders in 1569 and later remodelled during Aurangzeb's rule. Since it stands on the Delhi-Jaipur route it has great strategic importance.

Bishop Heber, who visited Amber in 1825, paid glowing tribute to the grandeur of Amber: "I have seen many royal palaces containing larger and more stately rooms... but for varied and picturesque effects, for the richness of carving, for wild beauty of situation, for the number and romantic singularity of the apartments, and the strangeness of finding such a building in such a place and country I am able to compare nothing with Amber... I could not help thinking what magnificent use Ariosto or Sir Walter Scott would have made of such a building."

Opposite page: Top: Diwan-i-Khas or Sheesh Mahal, Amber Fort, Jaipur. Bottom: The fabulous lattice screens, Jas Mandir, Amber Fort, Jaipur.

Jaigarh Perched on the crest of hills of the ancient Dhundhar terrain is Jaigarh fort, four hundred feet above Amber. Once the stronghold of the Mina tribes, the summit provides a bird's-eye view of the barren hills where only eagles dared to roam. It was suitably called *Chilh ka tola* (hill of the eagle). Jaigarh has always been a military fort with no fancy architecture. Mirza Raja Jai Singh I and Jai Singh II built the towering fortification spurred by secret fears of a Mughal attack. But the fort was never stormed by enemy and its strength has remained a mere warning to ambitious rulers.

Jaivan, the world's largest and most magnificent cannon is Jaigarh's chief attraction. Jaivan has a 20 feet long barrel, richly ornamented with floral designs and animal figures. Weighing 50 tons, the front wheels have a diameter of nine and a half feet. Cast in the Jaigarh foundry in 1720, Jaivan was test-fired only once, when the cannon ball fell some 38 kilometres away, creating the most thunderous sound and causing many houses in Jaipur to collapse. The Jaigarh ramparts display many other grand cannons abandoned to the elements.

At such a great height water has always been a problem. Jaigarh has three underground tanks to store rain water. The largest tank has the capacity to store fifteen million gallons and is covered by a roof resting on pillars. The interior is pitchdark. Light a candle and it makes only darkness visible. The steps seem to descend into a cool vacuum. Mysterious and frightening even today, this tank, according to legend, contained within its dark interiors the fabulous treasures of the Kachhwaha rulers since Man Singh I. In 1976, the government of India took up excavations, using the latest gadgets to unearth the wealth. This six-month-long exercise proved fruitless, but gave currency to another myth: the hidden treasures had moved away into the bowels of the earth. Or, what is more possible, that Jai Singh II exhausted the wealth accumulated over the centuries on the building of Jaipur city.

Diwa Burj is the tower for keeping vigil over the neighbouring hills. It provides the most spectacular views of the meandering fortifications below, with Jaipur city on the right and the long narrow ribbon-like road to Delhi on the left.

The northern part of Jaigarh begins at Jaleb Chowk, near the tanks. The closed verandahs now house the museum displaying a bewildering variety of ancient treasury locks, oil and wine containers, rare maps of Amber and a few other objects of medieval armoury. At the cannon and gun foundry, established by Bhagwan Das in 1584, were cast many great cannons, much to the displeasure of the Delhi overlords who had kept the use of gunpowder a secret with them. The cannons on display are metallurgical marvels, and were put to frequent use in battles fought by Amber rulers.

Right: Jagat Shiromani Temple, Amber City, Jaipur. Far right: Sculptures on the marble columns at Jagat Shiromani Temple, Amber. Opposite page, Above: Ganesh Pol, entrance ot the royal enclosure, Amber Fort. Left: Visitors to the city of Jaipur.

The small shrine of Kal Bhairav still contains the original image in black metal. It is the presiding deity at Jaigarh. Some palaces, like the Diwan-i-Aam and Khilawat Niwas are small structures, architecturally uninspiring, but of great functional value. The vast courtyards make these structures look still smaller. Then, through a maze of secret passages, vaulted and dark, appears Vilas Mandir, sets of rooms, with vestibules opening into spacious courtyards and, at the extreme end, the grand *baradari* with a magnificent Mughal-style garden. This is the most splendid portion of Jaigarh.

From the western corner towers, you can see the engineering marvels of medieval Amber, a network of pipes and channels emanating from Sagar Talao, the water reservoir which sustained life at Jaigarh. From the eastern corner, the whole of Amber lies below and the grand palace lies as a table-top decoration, a rare but grand view of the city.

Nahargarh The fort of Nahargarh, earlier called Sudarshangarh, stands at the end of the hill range overlooking Jaipur city. A metalled road on the cleared hill top takes you into the interior of this fort, which was built by Sawai Jai Singh in 1734. It has an interesting legend. The entire day's work was being regularly demolished at night by some forces. The king met someone who revealed the secret. The land belonged to a dead *bhomia* (owner of the tract) called Nahar Singh and the king had to appease the dead man's soul if he wanted to make progress. Nahar Singh was assigned a small fortress near Purana Ghat and a small shrine was built at Jaigarh for regular homage to his soul.

Nahargarh has only one palace, in fact a double-storeyed set of interconnected suites for ladies of the harem. The rooms are beautifully washed in pale cream and dado panels carry restrained ornamentation. Ram Singh II made some additions to the palace in 1868-69 and Madho Singh II further built some extensions in 1902-3. It is believed that some treasure was kept here but was later shifted to Moti Doongri Palace in the city by Man Singh II. The ramparts and bastions are still majestic and of great strategic strength.

Jaipur When Jai Singh II, as a thirteen-year-old prince was presented before Aurangzeb, the haughty Mughal dispensed with courtesy and rudely asked his young visitor: "Your

Right: Jaigarh Fort, crowning the hill overlooking Amber Fort, Jaipur. Opposite page, Top: The city of Jaipur lies below the towering ramparts of the Nahargarh Fort. Below, Left: Jaivan, the world's largest cannon cast at the Jaigarh foundry. Right: A fresco panel in the courtyard of Nahargarh Fort.

ancestors gave me much trouble. Now say what you deserve of me before saying what you desire." And to shock the lad out of his wits, grabbed his hands and glowered over him. "Tell me, what use are your arms now?" he asked.

The prince answered: "Your Majesty, when a bridegroom takes his bride's hand in one of his own during the wedding, he is bound by duty to protect her all his life. Now that the Emperor of India has taken my hand in his right hand, what have I to fear? With Your Majesty's long arms to protect me, what other arms do I need?" For a moment Aurangzeb was left dumb struck at the wisdom and audacity of the lad, but he was pleased with the retort. He admitted him as 'Sawai'(one and a quarter) over his contemporaries. Jai Singh II was titled Sawai Jai Singh II and lived long at the Mughal court to prove his worth.

Sawai Jai Singh II soon became known as the most enlightened ruler of the Kachhwaha clan, in contrast to Jai Singh I, the Mirza Raja. Sawai Jai Singh II was not a great soldier, certainly not the stuff Rajput heroes are made of but "his talents for civil government and court intrigue, in which he was the Machiavelli of his day, were at that period far more notable auxiliaries," says James Todd, the historian, summing up his character.

Sawai Jai Singh II wielded great influence during the rule of Muhammad Shah II, who presided over the disintegration of Mughal power in India. The weak Mughal king was no hindrance to Sawai's own plans to enlarge his Amber territories and build a new city. In 1725, the Amber Raja issued orders for the building of Jai Niwas in the plains below the Nahargarh hill. This was to be the nucleus of the new city. In 1727, construction work started in full swing and the massive fortifications and grand gateways rose to their full height. A canal was dug to ensure a perennial water supply.

Vidyadhar Bhattacharya, a descendant of a family of priests from Bengal imported by Man Singh I, was the chief architect. Well versed in the Shilpashastras, Vidyadhar chose a grid pattern for planning the city building flanking straight and wide roads. Between Suraj Pol and Chand Pol stretched the city, divided into eight squares or *nidhis* (signifying the treasures of the lord of wealth and prosperity) and the City Palace formed the ninth square. Traders and businessmen from distant places were invited to settle down in Jaipur and practised their particular trade, so some city areas came to be identified with the specialized trade practised there. On the wide thoroughfares six or seven carriages could drive abreast with ease and the visitor could wonder at the magnificent palaces, temples and markets on both sides. Even today the roads can conveniently contain the procession of pandemonium—cars, taxis, scooters, buses, bullock-carts, trucks, camel carts, cycle rickshaws, cyclists, pedestrians, and hawkers. Ram Singh II had the city painted in pink, his idea of welcoming the Prince of Wales in 1876. Since then, Jaipur or Jainagar has earned the popular sobriquet—the Pink City.

The City Palace or Chandra Mahal forms the core of the city. In fact, it stands surrounded by various smaller structures meant for officials and guests. As with the Mughals, the private residential block is concealed behind high curtain walls and imposing gateways. Courtyards, large and spacious, stand at the centre of the building complexes.

The Sire Deorhi Gate and Naqqar Khana Gate were the original entrances to the palace. Now you pass through the Gainda Ka Deorhi (Rhinoceros Gate) to enter a courtyard surrounded by a double-storeyed row of rooms with balconies. At the centre stands Mubarak Mahal, an excellently designed guesthouse with the beauty of a jewel box. It housed the Textile Museum, displaying rare items of *zari*, block prints, royal dresses in splendid silks, and brocades embroidered with gorgeous designs. An attraction here is the fabulous huge dress in pink silk worn by Madho Singh I (1750-68), who was also nearly 7 feet tall and weighed some 496 pounds (225 kg). Also to be seen are some obsolete musical instruments. Architecturally Mubarak Mahal is a very ornamental structure with slender pillars and exquisitely carved balconies.

Quite surprisingly, Ram Singh II, one of the Jaipur rulers, was a keen amateur photographer. His photographs of contemporary Jaipur are displayed at Silah Khana, near Mubarak Mahal. He also introduced modern facilities to the city such as a Public Works Department (1860), State Postal System on camels (1861), a Municipality (1868), pipe lines for water supply (1874) and street lighting.

Sarhad ki Deorhi is the lovely gateway to the City Palace. Its central arch is flanked by two elephant statues in white marble. The splendid bronze door, kept shining by attendants, is a piece of beauty. The guards, suitably attired in white long coats and a red turban, are always in demand for a souvenir photograph.

Beyond Sarhad ki Deorhi is yet another courtyard, at the centre of which stands the Diwan-i-Khas on a podium. It is a simple but functional structure of a double row of marble pillars supporting engrailed arches. On display here are two huge silver urns which Madho Singh II carried with him to England in 1901. He was the first Kachhwaha ruler to go abroad and carried Ganges water to avoid drinking the *firangipani* of the Thames. Each urn can store 1800 gallons of water and 2427 kg (535 pounds) of silver was required to cast each one.

The Ridhi Sidhi Pol, a four-storeyed structure, stands framed within the City Palace wall, and through a staggered entrance leads to Pritam Chowk, the grandest courtyard, lying immediately below the City Palace. The eastern and western walls contain four marvellous frescoed doorways, kept in perfect condition since they form part of the present ex-Maharaja's private property. These doorways, painted under the directions of Pratap Singh (1778-1803), depict the moods of the four Indian seasons. The door used for entrance from Ridhi Sidhi Pol is the one most fabulously decorated with the gorgeous peacock motifs in turquoise, blue, amber and aquamarine.

On the northern side of Pritam Chowk stands Chandra Mahal or City Palace, a grand seven-storeyed structure majestically rising to a commanding height. The original ground floor structure contains a hall displaying the portraits of Jaipur rulers. Particularly attractive is the gold work on the ceiling and an exquisitely carved brass door depicting scenes from the Krishna Leela. The upper floors were added subsequently by other rulers. Mukut Mahal the topmost pavilion, is in marble and has an attractive curvilinear roof. The City Palace provides ramps instead of the regular stairs. This was to facilitate the easy movement of palanquins and wheelchairs in which a particular Maharaja afflicted with rheumatism could move about conveniently.

The varied styles in the palace reflect the taste and sophistication of the rulers who built them. Some beautiful portions of the palace are in actual use by the present ex-Maharaja, Lt. Col. Bhawani Singh and hence closed to the public. Chabi Niwas has an exquisite palace painted in Wedgewood blue, complete with white lining.

Through the ground floor doors you can see the garden stretching upto Govind Devji's temple. The temple building was actually being used by Sawai Jai Singh II as his first residence in Jaipur till he had a vision instructing him to leave the building as it was a dwelling for God. He installed a Krishna image brought from Mathura at the temple and moved into Chandra Mahal. The garden and the water channel add grandeur to the palaces besides providing greenery in this dry desert city.

Back in the Diwan-i-Khas square, you must visit the museum housed in the Diwan-i-Aam at the north-eastern corner. On display are specimens of rare miniature paintings of Rajasthan, manuscripts of Sawai Jai Singh II's work on astronomy, and Abul Fazl's translation of the *Mahabharata* called *Razmnamah*. Many translations of rare books, illustrated with the most exquisite miniatures are real treasures. The carpets from Herat, Lahore and Agra still look magnificent. The old palanquins and howdahs used by the Maharajas of yore are still objects of great interest. The Diwan-i-Aam treasures need to be better displayed as this small hall is literally crammed with articles of great antiquity and unequalled craftsmanship.

Hawa Mahal To the north of Badi Chaupad stands Hawa Mahal, the landmark of Jaipur and the best known monument of fanciful architecture. Built by Sawai Pratap Singh, the aesthete among Maharajas (1778-1803), it is part of the City Palace, though standing away from the main complex. At first glance it seems to be whimsical in design. From the roadside, from where most of the visitors look at it, Hawa Mahal looks a mere facade. But there is much more to it than meets the eye. Actually, it is the last portion of an extensive *Zenana* palace meant for the royal ladies, a palace of winds away from the claustrophobic surroundings of a palace guarded by battalions of liveried guards. Heat, the main problem of Rajasthan cities, causes little irritation at Hawa Mahal. From the small latticed windows ladies could watch the processions on the street without fear of being observed by the common man. Queens, princesses and courtesans were thus provided a concealed grandstand view. The palace has a regular courtyard with all the sides lined with suites and apartments. The upper storeys are reached through a ramp instead of regular stairs, a device to facilitate movement for the less athletic type.

Opposite page, Top: Hawa Mahal, Jaipur. Below, Left: Ridhi Sidhi Pol, City Palace, Jaipur. Right: View of the city from the top of Hawa Mahal, Jaipur.

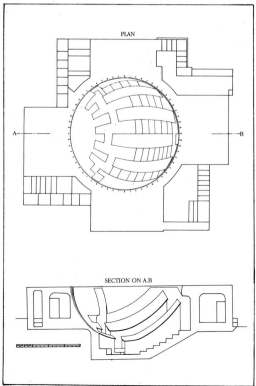

PLAN

A — B

SECTION ON A.B

Some critics have condemned Hawa Mahal as "a baroque folly" and "a bizarre" piece of architecture. The five-storeyed facade, encrusted with excellent *jali* work and small balconies, has 953 niches and is only one room deep. Lal Chand Ustad, who designed the Hawa Mahal, dedicated it to Radha and Krishna, but its elaborate and fanciful structure appealed to the fancy of the ruler who thought it more useful as a palace for pleasures for the ladies than as a mere temple. The pyramidal outline of the structure has one characteristic feature of Jaipur architecture – symmetry. "The forms employed are familiar enough, but the bays are crammed together, piled and multiplied so that they combine to form a larger version of themselves, in a manner strikingly reminiscent of a temple shikhara."

The Mughals built some pleasure palaces such as Panch Mahal at Sikri and Musamman Burj at Agra fort, but Hawa Mahal has the most highly imaginative design. The curvilinear roof, domes and finials contribute the charm of quaintness which makes Hawa Mahal look so exotic and Oriental. From the top floor, the city of Jaipur lies spread out before the eyes: the straight wide roads and the teeming crowds in the market, Jantar Mantar, City Palace and Nahargarh fort are all identifiable on the expansive vista.

Sir Edwin Arnold thought Hawa Mahal was "a vision of daring and dainty loveliness, of storeys of rosy masonry and delicate overhanging balconies and latticed windows. Soaring with tier after tier of fanciful architecture in a pyramidal form, a very mountain of airy and audacious beauty through the thousand peirced screens and gilded arches of which the Indian air blows cool over the flat roofs of the very highest house. Alladin's magician could have called into existence no more marvellous abode."

The beauty of Hawa Mahal lies in its fragile appearance which, like a vision, threatens to vanish into thin air. It is of Jaipur's buildings, the most romantic and delicate.

Jantar Mantar To a visitor uninitiated in the science of astronomy the various masonry instruments built near the City Palace might appear interesting but confusing, a set for a science fiction movie. But these instruments are the most precise modes of studying the movements of the sun and calculations of time: "These futuristic instruments have a surreal, abstract beauty. Walking into the observatory is like stepping into some lunar landscape... but there is nothing abstract about these massive geometric instruments."

The builder of these scientific instruments was Sawai Jai Singh II, who was a great scholar of astronomy and pursued his experiments despite diplomatic engagements. The Mughal empire under Muhammad Shah II was fast declining in power and the Marathas were causing quite some trouble at Agra and Delhi. His growing disenchantment with the politics of power led him towards astronomical studies with redoubled vigour. He has invited scholars from Bavaria, France and Portugal for consultations and they brought with them the latest astronomical researches from abroad. Jai Singh II found, the popular astronomical tables defective. The results of his experiments with brass instruments proved unsatisfactory. Even the use of instruments like those of Ulugh Begh in Samarkand did not yield precise readings.

At home, Jai Singh II was guided in his researches by Pandit Jagannath, Kewal Ram and Vidyadhar Bhattacharya. Muhammad Shah II gave Jai Singh II all the encouragement in his work "for ascertaining of the point in question," as he had already built observatories at Delhi, Mathura, Varanasi and Ujjain. At Jaipur, Jai Singh II built instruments in stone and white marble for a greater and more precise reading. He worked out a set of tables dedicated to the Mughal king.

The observatory at Jaipur was the last and was built between 1728-34. A few details about some important instruments are as follows:

Samrat Yantra (Large). This is the most accurate instrument at the observatory. It is the largest sun dial in the world. The gnomon is 90 feet in height and very accurate in finding the time and declination. The arches cut in the gnomon wall ensure perfect stability and correctness in results. The graduated edges and arcs help the findings without fault. Even the monsoon can be predicted with readings at this Samrat Yantra and "from reading the position of the dot of light, the altitude, declination, zenith and distance of the sun can be seen. The variation in the sun's diameter can also be accurately measured and even the sun spots could easily be observed." Jaipur's solar time was read at the Samrat Yantra. The quadrants on either side helped in reading of the hours, which were announced to the citizens from

Opposite page, Top: Jantar Mantar, with the City Palace and Nahargarh fort in the background, Jaipur. Bottom, Left: A section plan of Jai Prakash Yantra at Jantar Mantar, Jaipur. Right: Visitors at the Jantar Mantar, Jaipur.

the top of the steps. Since 1940 this practice has been stopped, although it continues to be a marvel of accuracy.

Jai Prakash Yantra. This is the showpiece of Jai Singh's researches. It is used for measuring the rotation of the sun. The two hemispherical cavities are complementary, forming one complete hemisphere if joined together. It is used in finding out the sun's longitude and latitude and the sign of the zodiac through which it is passing. The two instruments are interconnected at the basement. The ingenious designs are not only attractive but greatly instructive, particularly to the young students of this science.

Ram Yantra. It is instrumental in finding out zenith distance and the altitude of the sun. These two complementary buildings are also useful in studying the movement of the stars and making weather forecasts. In fact, what the Jai Prakash achieves with a sunken hemisphere, the Ram Yantra achieves with an upright structure.

Rashvalayas Yantra. There are twelve small sun dials, one for each sign of the zodiac and are in fact, smaller versions of the Samrat Yantra.

Narivalaya Yantra. This sun dial can help determine local time in a simple, uncomplicated way.

Yantra Raj. This is the largest astrolab in the world – a brass disc, seven feet in diameter that can be moved in a vertical plane. Calculations for the Hindu calendar, festivals and other religious calculations have been based on the Yantra Raj readings for the last 250 years.

There are many other instruments which are of unchallengeable accuracy, the greatest gift of Jai Singh II to Indian studies in science.

Gaitore Gaitore is one of the most picturesque spots in Jaipur. It is an enclosed area at the foot of Nahargarh hill containing the cenotaphs of the rulers of Jaipur which are built on the cremation sites, surrounded by high hills and covered in seclusion.

Largely, these cenotaphs follow a similar construction plan and proportions to the *Paanchayatana* style, i.e., the central domed pavilion raised on slender pillars, with a high terrace and four subsidiary ornamental pavilions at the corners. The cenotaph of Sawai Madho Singh II is the largest and has the most lavishly ornamental ceiling. It looks very majestic and is a charming example of memorial architecture.

The cenotaph of Sawai Jai Singh II is a gem of architecture, with a ceiling exquisitely sculptured in the style of the Dilwara temples at Mt. Abu. It has an elegance characteristic of the man as of the city he built. Panels on the plinth depict battle scenes taken from life, elephant fights and floral decorations, executed with remarkable craftsmanship. Also well worth a close look are the cenotaphs of Ram Singh II and Madho Singh I, the giant ruler of Jaipur

The Lake Palace stands at the centre of a green oasis. It was built by Madho Singh I in the midst of the Man Sagar Lake which is now completely dry except for a few days during the monsoons. The bed of the lake is now used as a playground. The Lake Palace is not a pleasure palace, but only a palatial facade, and a blind for duck shooting. A little distance away from the Lake Palace stand the cenotaphs of some Maharanis, elegant and ornate structures in marble where nature seems to have overtaken the work of man. These cenotaphs for the Maharajas and Maharanis are extremely beautiful structures, but unlike the Mughal garden tombs, stand deserted, visited only by a few.

Galta The Galta hilltop offers a spectacular view of Jaipur. Galta one of the prime seats of the Ramanand seat of the Vaishnovites, is associated with the sage Galva who performed his penance here. The seven tombs filled in the water flowing from the stone-carved cow-mouthed, are held sacred by the devotees and are believed to have curative properties. The terraces are lined with pavilions decorated with charming murals. The two hayelies at the foot of the Galta hill are presently used as temples. There exterior is covered with lavish frescoed decorations, mostly depicting legends from the life of Krishna. The haveli close to the tea-shop has an over-hanging balcony covering really stunning decorations with exiquisite floral motifs executved in the style of miniature paintings. Yet another delopidated haveli has a gorgeosly painted lotus ceiling.

The sun temple on the crest of the Galta hill is the only one of its kind here, to remind that the Kachhwaha rulers of Jaipur are Surya vanshies descendant of the Sun. From this end a

Opposite page, top: Lake Palace, Jaipur. Bottom, left: Secred pool at Galtaji. Right: Gaitore cenotaph of Madhosingh II.

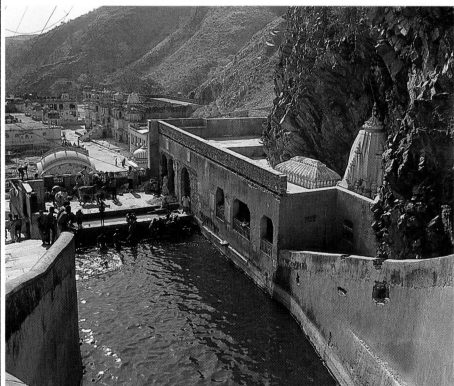

narrow ribbon-path winds its way down the hill which is a short cut to city.

The Purana Ghat contains two splendid gardens. The Sisodia Rani's Palace and Garden was built for the Udaipur princess, wife of Sawai Jai Singh II who had demanded a separate royal residence for herself and the right of succession to the Jaipur seat for her son. Here was born Madho Singh I. The luxuriantly laid out terraced gardens with water channels and fountains are set amid spectacular hills, so reminiscent of the Mughal gardens in Kashmir. The small but tastefully laid out garden of Vidyadhar, the architect of Jaipur, has a charming setting to which the towering granite hills add a touch of the picturesque.

Coming back to the city, you must ask to be shown, if only from a distance, the Moti Doongri Palace, the hilltop fortress of Maharani Gayatri Devi. It resembles in shape a pearl, but is generally called the "Scottish folly" by those who find its architectural style weirdly outlandish. Its looks exude an aura of mystery and romance.

The major educational institutions of Jaipur, the University, Medical College, and Government Secretariat buildings are all located near this new area of the city that has developed around the Statue Circle.

Among the beautiful garden palaces of Jaipur, the Rambagh Palace holds a prominent place. It was once the retreat of royalty and Ram Singh II used it to play a game of billiards. Later, Madho Singh II sought the help of Sir Swinton Jacob to transform it into a royal playground complete with a swimming pool, tennis and squash courts, etc. Man Singh II made his own additions and converted it into a residential palace fitted with the latest conveniences for a modern Maharaja. The City Palace no longer met his requirements of luxury and privacy and love for outdoor sports, particularly polo, for which he won world-wide acclaim. He named the palace after his ancestor.

Today Ram Bagh Palace is a five-star hotel, a royal setting with grand architecture, towers, turrets, cupolas, pavilions, corridors, terraces, large banquet halls and sprawling lawns. The decor is typically Rajasthani and gives a glimpse of the splendour that surrounded the lives of Jaipur's Maharajas.

The Ram Niwas Gardens were also laid out by Ram Singh II, but were later relaid to accommodate the requirements of space in a fast growing city. Albert Hall stands majestically in this park which contains the zoological park as well.

This is a small sea of greenery in Jaipur which is otherwise surrounded by barren hills and encroaching sands.

Central Museum Albert Hall, housing the central museum, stands in the Ram Niwas Garden. Built by Ram Singh II to commemorate the Jaipur visit by Prince of Wales in 1876, the Albert Hall was designed by Sir Swinton Jocob. The structure modelled after the Victoria and Albert Museum in London is remarkable for its use of marble with sandstone, lovely kiosks, curvilinear eaves, pink balustrades and open courtyards enclosed within arcaded passages.

The museum contains a vast treasure of art, textiles, metalware, jewellery, coin, pottery, sculpture and miniature paintings. Within the display galleries are kept some rare specimens of embossed, hammered and charge brasswork on shields, plaques and salvers. The carpets from Herat are rare and magnificent.

Sanganer Lying 15 kms south-east of Jaipur, Sanganer is legendary for its beautiful block printed textiles. It has a fortified wall skirting the town and a few strong gateways. It was at Sanganer where Sawai Jai Singh II imprisoned his younger brother, the rebellious Vijay Singh.

The river Amani Shah flows through the town. Bundles of cloth dyed in various hues lie spread out on the sand for quick drying. Sanganer has been famous for block printing and paper making. Screen printing of textiles is a comparatively new but very popular occupation.

The typical Sanganer print is made on a pale yellow or brown cotton and the floral designs are classic in character, which has remained unchanged for centuries.

Opposite page, Top: Rambagh Palace, Jaipur. Bottom, Left: A pujari at a temple on the road to Galtaji, Jaipur. Right: Cloth printing at Sanganer, near Jaipur Following page: Sheesh Mahal Glass Mosaic, Amber Fort, Jaipur.

Glossary

AZAN: *muezzim's call for prayer at the mosque.*

BARADARI: *a pillared portico or pavilion, usually in open courtyard or garden.*

BAGH: *garden.*

BAOLI: *stepwell often elaborately decorated, also used as a cool retreat during the summer months.*

CHAR-BAGH: *a Persian garden divided into four parts by paths & watercourses.*

CHAJJA: *deep eaves, used for providing shade & protection from rain over doors & windows.*

CHATTRI: *a domed octagonal kiosk cenotaph, most frequently used in Rajasthan, a decorative feature in Mughal architecture.*

DOUBLE DOME: *a dome with two layers. The inner shell covers the interior, the outer shell gives the impression of increased height, with a space between the layers.*

HAMMAM: *bathing place/apartments. turkish Bath. The Mughals used the cool interior for secret parlays & for convivial parties.*

HAREM: *female members of the royal household.*

HOWDAHS: *elaborate seat on elephant back.*

JALI: *fretted lattice elaborately carved marble or stone slabs for providing cover while admitting light & air.*

JHAROKHA DARSHAN: *ceremonial public appearance on a projected balcony.*

MINAR: *minaret, tower.*

MIHRAB: *arched alcove, prayer niche of a mosque facing used towards the Qibla for the direction of Mecca.*

MIMBAR: *pulpit in a mosque.*

OGEE: *'S' shaped apex of the arch.*

ODHNI: *colourful head covering used by women.*

POL: *gateway.*

PANCHAYATANA: *temple with four subsidiary corner shrines grouped around a central one.*

PIETRA DURA: *inlaid mosaic of precious stones.*

SERAI: *public inn, halting place.*

SHILPASHASTRA: *ancient texts on architecture & sculpture.*

SHIKHARA: *the tower over the sanctum of the temple.*

SQUINCH ARCH: *arches placed diagonally at the angles in the interior domes to convert from square to round.*

TORANA: *architrave.*

ZENANA: *women's quarters in Muslim palaces.*

Photo credit:

Surendra Sahai: 11, 12, 14, 15, 16 (bottom left & right), 19 (bottom), 21, 23, 25, 31, 32-33, 34, 35, 38, 39, 41 (bottom), 42, 43, 45, 46, 49, 52, 54, 55, 59, 60 (bottom), 62, 64-65, 66, 68, 75, 76, 78, 79, 80, 81, 82-83, 84, 87, 88, 91, 92 (bottom), 94-95.

Thomas Dix: Cover, 16 (top), 19 (top), 22, 50-51, 55 (top), 56-57, 60 (top), 72-73, Back cover.

Rupinder Khullar: 6, 26-27, 40, 41 (top), 53, 69, 74, 92 (top).

Robert Huber: 4-5.

Ashwani Sabharwal: 2-3.